Investigating TECHNOLOGY BOOK 3

Robert Fisher & John Garvey

SIMON & SCHUSTER
EDUCATION

Text© Robert Fisher and John Garvey 1992
Design © Simon & Schuster 1992
Artwork© The illustrators credited 1992

First published in 1992 in Great Britain by
Simon & Schuster Education
Campus 400
Maylands Avenue
Hemel Hempstead HP2 7EZ

Printed in Great Britain by
Dotesios Ltd
Trowbridge

British Library Cataloguing in Publication Data
A catalogue record of this book is available from the British
Library

ISBN 0 7501 0222 5

Series Editor John Day
Edited by John Morton
Designed by Jerry Watkiss/Kingsway Advertising
Artwork by Robert and Rhoda Burns (8, 12, 13, 16, 21, 22, 23,
25, 28, 30, 32, 33, 37, 40, 41, 42, 43, 44, 46)
Anna Hancock (15, 17, 19, 27, 29, 31)
Brian Hoskin/Simon Girling & Associates (9, 39, 45, 47)
Mike Lacey/Simon Girling & Associates (11)
Shirley Wheeler and Fineline Partners (35)
Cover artwork by Jerry Watkiss
Typeset by Kelvin Meadows/Kingsway Advertising

Contents

Introduction

Investigating Technology contains a collection of problem solving activities for use in primary and middle schools.

- Books 1 and 2 are intended for the 6 – 10 age range (Years 2 – 5).
- Books 3 and 4 are intended for the 8 – 12 age range (Years 4 – 7).

The activities chosen are relevant to children of different ages and abilities at Key Stage 2 in the National Curriculum.

Selection for each book has been based on:

a) the notion of the spiral curriculum in which skills and concepts are 'revisited' through ascending levels of attainment

b) the need to introduce in Books 1 and 2 the skills and techniques required for activities in Books 3 and 4.

There are ten themes that run through the four books. These appear alphabetically as:

- Buildings
- Clothes
- Communication
- Conservation
- Food
- Home
- Recreation
- School
- Transport
- World of Work

Each book contains 20 units or problem solving challenges, two for each theme. A unit consists of a double-page spread of teacher's notes and pupil's worksheet which may be photocopied for use in school. Each unit presents a design challenge to children, suitable for individual, group or class work. The investigations have been chosen and classroom-tested to provide a stimulating design challenge requiring the use of technological skills and concepts. There is a Techniques section in each book to offer support for teachers and pupils, as well as resource sheets and a record sheet, which may also be photocopied.

Investigating Technology has been designed to meet National Curriculum requirements, and to enrich any school scheme for design and technology. The suggested activities may be adapted to suit the needs of individual teachers and of individual children. The series is a flexible resource which:

- provides a rich source of stimulating design and technology activities
- can involve pupils in investigations of their own choice
- is suitable for group work on a particular theme
- offers ideas and starting points for class teaching
- fits naturally into either cross-curricular work or subject-based teaching
- provides ideas and stimulus for further activity in design and technology.

The Teacher's Notes suggest starting points, materials to be used, a context for each activity, stimulus questions to aid investigation, techniques for designing and making, and ways of extending the investigation. The units are cross-referred to show links, continuities and developments in related investigations. The activities can be developed in different ways to provide design and technology experience at many levels.

The Pupil's Pages offer a theme and a challenge within a design process which reflects the Attainment Targets (ATs) set out in the National Curriculum.

The design process can be illustrated as follows:

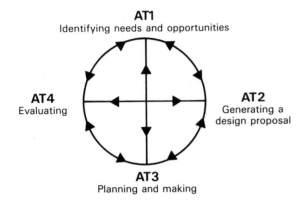

The Pupil's Pages aim to reflect this process as follows:

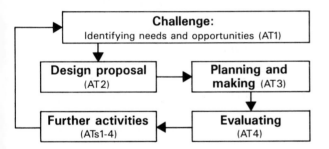

The design of the Pupil's Pages should not be regarded as a rigid framework, but rather as a set of reminders as to what might be involved in a child's investigation. Note that children can start at any point in the design process, beginning, for example, by evaluating a product and seeking their own ways to improve it. Each Pupil's Page begins with a challenge which offers one way into the design process by identifying a need and opportunity for technological activity (AT1). Because the subject matter of design and technology is so wide, and can be related to all human activity, there is no content specified for it in the National Curriculum. Each activity in this book is designed to meet National Curriculum requirements by developing tasks which allow children to meet all four attainment targets:

- giving children freedom to identify needs and opportunities (AT1)
- encouraging them to produce their own design proposal, and to develop it into an appropriate and achievable design specification (AT2)

- planning and making artefacts, systems and environments (see diagram below), encouraging them to identify, manage and use appropriate material and resources and to work to a plan in making chosen items (AT3)
- developing, communicating and acting upon an evaluation of the processes, products and effects of their activities (AT4).

What the attainment targets set out is the *process* through which children can attain design and technology capability.

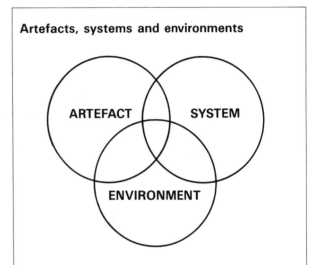

Artefacts, systems and environments

If they are to achieve design and technology capability, children need practice in designing and making:

- **artefacts** different sorts of objects made by people, such as jewellery, a container, a shelter, a vehicle, furniture

- **systems** a set of objects and activities designed to perform a task, such as a business enterprise, road routes, party plans, recycling project, distribution system

- **environments** surroundings made or developed by people, such as an adventure playground, wildlife garden, housing estate, interior design, animal home

Artefacts, systems and enviroments can be interrelated: for example, a car is an artefact (object), a system (set of objects) and an environment (surrounding people).

Design and technology capability

Technology challenges pupils (and teachers) to apply their knowledge and skills to solve practical problems. It is more than just the process of making 'hardware', of making things like cars and bridges. Rather it is about identifying and answering human needs, generating ideas, planning, making and testing to find the best solutions. Through activity in design and technology, children can learn how to explore, control and improve aspects of their own environment: for example, how to have a healthy diet or to recycle waste materials. Technology is to do with capability, giving children the 'know how' to answer their own needs, and the needs of others in a given context or environment. It is also about developing a reflective understanding of issues related to how technology shapes and is shaped by society. These two distinct aspects of capability in design and technology need to work together as children tackle a task.

The two aspects of capability are:

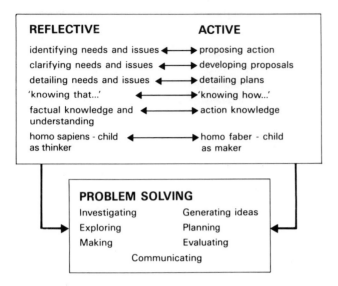

The aims of teaching technology might be summarised as follows:

- *extending capability or 'know how',* developing children's practical abilities in designing, making and problem solving, and stimulating their originality and enterprise
- *extending understanding of how technology and society influence each other, relating technology to social change,* increasing awareness of the way technology is changing our homes, workplaces and lifestyles, and of the factors that influence technological development such as economic, social and political processes.

Becoming technologically literate or capable means coming to grips with the problems of living in, and exerting influence upon, the constructed world.

In the National Curriculum, technology is divided into two aspects (or profile components):

- design and technology capability
- information technology capability

The focus of these books is on the first of these, although reference is made to the important role information technology can play in supporting the process of investigation. Types of software that can support design and technology include programs for:

- *communicating information:* for example, wordprocessing of design proposals, plans and evaluations
- *handling information:* for example, databases used to store, list and explore factual details related to topics under investigation
- *modelling:* for example, graphics programs for visually 'modelling' designs of artefacts to be made, such as badges, bookmarks, vehicles, furniture or clothes
- *measurement and control:* for example, Control Logo used to control models such as traffic lights, model machines and warning systems.

Each investigation will offer opportunities to consider and explore the applications and effects of information technology (IT).

The reference to capabilty emphasises that technology is a subject concerned with practical action related to a wide range of other subjects. Traditionally technology has been associated with science, and design with art or craft. How does technology differ from science? Science is about exploring the physical world, and answers questions such as 'How does it behave?' and 'Why does it happen?' Design and technology are about controlling the environment to achieve particular purposes, and answers questions such as 'How can we design/make something that will ...'

Some differences between technology and science

TECHNOLOGY INVOLVES	SCIENCE INVOLVES
thinking about processes	thinking about causes
successful products	explanation and prediction
practical invention	theoretical discovery
design	analysis
searches for solutions	searches for causes
research for practical purposes	research for its own sake
study of how things might be	study of things as they are

Scientific principles will be involved in any technological activity. Ways in which design and technology relate to different subject areas include:

- English – expression and communication of ideas through reading, writing, talking and listening
- maths – shape (2-D and 3-D), measurement, data handling, applications and analysis
- science – principles applied to materials, structures, energy, mechanisms and control
- history – designing and making artefacts, systems and environments from the past
- geography – designing and making artefacts, systems and environments from other places and cultures
- art – aesthetic response, visual thinking, graphic design, use of art/craft techniques
- music – designing and making musical artefacts, systems and environments
- PE – designing sequences of physical activity, and artefacts relating to physical pursuits
- RE – designing and making artefacts and organising celebrations relating to religious customs and festivals.

Technology can be taught through topics, projects or units of study, which link with other National Curriculum subjects, and with cross-curricular themes such as :

- *economic and industrial understanding:* for example, through studying the needs of local business, or setting up a mini-enterprise, evaluating costs and benefits
- *environmental education:* for example, through studying ways of improving the local environment, conservation of natural resources and improving the quality of life
- *health education:* for example, through planning healthy systems and environments, such as promoting hygiene and healthy diets
- *safety education:* for example, through learning the need for safety procedures, the correct use of tools, and the creation of safe artefacts, systems and environments
- *education for citizenship:* for example, through learning the rights, responsibilities and duties of consumers, use

of public services and the values that underlie technological activity

- *multicultural education*: for example, through study of the artefacts, systems and environments of other cultures
- *personal and social education*: for example, caring for the needs of individuals and groups.

In developing their capability or 'know how', and in extending their understanding of the relationship between technology and society, children will need to identify design-and-make opportunities that relate to human needs in a variety of contexts. The following shows how possible contexts for technological activity relate to the major themes in this book:

CONTEXT	THEMES
Home	Home, Food
School	School, Communication
Recreation	Recreation, Clothes
Local community	Conservation, Buildings
Business and industry	Transport, World of Work

Children need experience of both real and imaginary contexts. Projects based on identifying needs in the local community provide opportunities for investigating real contexts. The use of stories such as 'The Lighthouse-keeper's Lunch' (see *Book 1* p10) or historical settings (see *Book 4* Castles) can offer imaginary contexts for design challenges. Developing a conservation area (*Book 4* p22) is an example of an activity that could relate to a real or imaginary context.*

The role of the teacher

The Teacher's Notes in each unit suggest ways of putting investigations into a meaningful context for learning to take place. In this sense, every teacher is a designer, choosing and creating the right conditions for children's learning. What kind of learning should this be?

As HMI suggest, 'active learning, and a sense of purpose and success, enhance pupil's enjoyment, interest, confidence and sense of personal worth; passive learning and inappropriate teaching styles can lead to frustration and failure.' The activites in this book can offer many opportunities for children to develop such active learning skills as:

A natural cycle of investigation will include some or all of these active learning processes. In addition there will be particular skills associated with the use of tools, materials and construction techniques for the doing and making stages. Useful craft skills needed to carry out the investigations are covered in the Techniques section.

The National Curriculum requires that children work with a range of materials, including:

- textiles
- graphic media, such as paint, paper, photographs
- construction materials, such as clay, wood, plastic, metal
- food.

For a recomended list of tools and resources, see Resources section p64.

An essential part of Design and Technology activities is that they should be carried out with due regard for safety in well organised working environments where children are trained in the use of tools and materials. Particular attention should be paid to the hygienic handling of food in a separate area of the classroom or school. Clear labelling and safe storage of resources is also important. ▲ printed beside 'materials' in the Teacher's Notes indicates an activity may involve potentially hazardous tools or materials.

The Programmes of Study for technology suggest that children themselves take responsibility for safety 'agreeing and following class rules for safe working'†. In considering the possible consequences of their design proposals, children should ask:

- Will it be safe?
- How will it affect others?

Other aspects of the role of the teacher include:

- preparing the learning environment (attractive displays, accessible materials etc)
- being a challenger, enabler and consultant during the learning process
- recording the work and evaluating progress (a sample record sheet on the inside back cover offers one way of recording achievement).††

Real design tasks come in many forms and in many time scales. This series aims to offer a diversity of challenges, starting points, and contexts to be explored. The greater the diversity of activities offered by the teacher, the richer will be the experience for children, both in developing skills and concepts, and in enjoyment and sense of achievement. As one young designer said, after much trial and error: 'I didn't know I could do it until I done it!'

*See also Problem Solving in Primary Schools, *edited by Robert Fisher, (Simon & Schuster Education) for examples of investigations in imaginary (p136ff) and real (p167ff) contexts.*

†*See* Be Safe – Some Aspects of Safety in School Science and Technology for Key Stages 1 and 2, *published by the Association for Science Education.*

††*See also* Recording Achievement in Primary Schools *by Robert Fisher (Simon & Schuster Education).*

Remote island shelter

Starting points

- Read a passage from *Robinson Crusoe* or another remote island story.
- Investigate maps showing possible locations of remote islands.
- Computer program 'Spanish Main' — the ship you are in control of is shipwrecked!

Materials ▲

Materials that might be washed up on a seashore (eg twigs, branches, string), Plasticine, clay, mirrors, atlases, plastic sheeting, compass.

Teaching notes

Discuss the context of the challenge. Encourage children to draw or model their own island showing realistic features. Children can choose a real island from a map as a stimulus for their own adventure.

The shelter is probably best built as small model that can be tested for rain and wind resistance. This can be used as a prototype for a full-scale version.

A device for catching small animals might be a hunting instrument or trap.

Key questions could include:
- What might be the size, shape and nature of the island?
- What things would we need to survive in all weathers?
- How could we protect ourselves from wild animals?
- What could we do to gather or grow food?
- What could we do to escape from the island?
- How could we record the passage of time?

Extension activities

- Make and keep a class diary of the sea voyage, shipwreck and life on the remote island. Small groups could contribute one day at a time in a continuous project. Children can design and make the book.
- Design, make and test rafts made from found materials.
- Study of history of famous voyages of discovery, eg Columbus, Cook, da Gama.

Related investigations

BUILDING AND STRUCTURES theme: *Book 1* Bridges p8, Lighthouse p10; *Book 2* Paper tower p8, Tent p10; *Book 3* Home of the future p10; *Book 4* Castles p8, Down on the farm p10. See also *Book 1* Minibeast trap p22; *Book 2* Pet home p20, Model boat p40; *Book 3* Making books p18.

Remote island shelter

Challenge

You are shipwrecked on a remote island. Can you devise a survival plan to keep you alive for at least seven days? You will need to build a shelter to keep you warm and dry.

Design proposal

- Think of how you can:
  - build a shelter
  - gather or hunt for food
  - collect fresh water
  - signal for help.
- What materials are you likely to find on the island?
- You can choose four out of the following ten items to bring with you:
  - a 5-litre can of water
  - a map of the ocean
  - a can of petrol
  - a transistor radio
  - 5 square metres of plastic sheet
  - a mirror
  - 6 m of rope
  - a box of chocolate bars
  - a compass
  - a pen-knife.

  List your choices and give reasons for them.

Evaluating

- Have you made a plan to keep you alive for seven days?
- Have you designed and made a shelter?
- Does your shelter keep you:
  - warm?
  - dry?
  - safe?
- Test your signalling device. Does it work by night and day?

Planning and making

- Draw ideas for your shelter.
- How will it protect you from wild animals?
- How will you use your chosen items?
- Can you make a device for catching:
  - animals?
  - fish?
- How will you collect and store fresh water?
- Can you design and make a device to signal for help?

Further activities

- How will you get off the island if no help arrives after seven days? Design and make something to help you escape. Test it out.
- Can you design and make a lifeboat to help you survive a shipweck? Include small items to put inside it to help you survive. Design and make a container for your survival kit.
- Make a model of your remote island. What features will you include?

Home of the future

Starting points
- Collect and study estate agents' advertising materials.
- Visit a house from the past. Compare and contrast it with the children's own homes.
- Discuss the future. What might life be like 100 years from now?

Materials ▲
Junk materials, cardboard, craft knives, cutting pads, graphic materials, printing materials and inks, Plasticine, marbling inks, large tray, newspaper, card, tie and dye equipment, brushes, fabric crayons, wood.

Teaching notes
Invite the children to design a questionnaire surveying the number of rooms, types of heating, colour of doors, number of lights and so on in each others' homes. This will encourage them to look closely at their own homes. Discuss what might change in the house of the future.

Children can work in groups, designing the whole house of the future or taking a single room. Attention should be paid to saving energy, recycling materials, the needs of others (eg there will be more old people as birth rates fall and medical care improves).

Discuss what can be learnt from the past in terms of:
- traditional crafts used in making furniture, design of wallpaper and so on
- use of energy
- shapes of roofs, rooms, windows.

Techniques
- Cardboard boxes form ideal starting points for the structure of the house or rooms (see Techniques p50).
- Special attention can be paid to:
  - wall-coverings. Consider marbling, printing or sten-cilling (see Techniques pp53, 58 and 59).
  - curtains and furniture coverings. Consider fabric crayons, fabric printing and tie and dye (see Techniques pp53, 57 and 61).
  - floor coverings. What will be the best surface?

Extension activities
- Analyse information gathered from the survey of children's homes using a database such as GRASS or OUR FACTS.
- Design and make a model garden for old people to use.
- Design and make a pulley system for a washing line.
- Investigate the history of a particular feature of houses, eg windows, heating systems.

Related investigations
BUILDING AND STRUCTURES theme: *Book 1* Bridges p8, Lighthouse p10; *Book 2* Paper tower p8, Tent p10; *Book 3* Remote island shelter p8; *Book 4* Castles p8, Down on the farm p10. See also *Book 3* Design a room p28.

Home of the future

Challenge

Can you design and make a model of a home of the future?

Design proposal

- How far ahead in the future will your home be?
- How many people will live in your home?
- What rooms will there be?
- What furniture will be in each room?
- What will be special about your house?
- Draw ideas for your home of the future.

Evaluating

- Show your model home to other people and explain what you have done.
- Is your home:
  - comfortable?
  - attractive to look at?
  - good for the environment?
  - different from a home of the present?
- Draw a diagram showing how and why it is different from your own home.
- Can you improve the home that you have made?

Planning and making

- What materials will you use to build your home?
- What ideas have you got for materials for making:
  - furniture?
  - stairs?
  - wall coverings?
  - furniture coverings?
  - curtains?
  - roofing?
  - lighting?
- How will you make them look attractive?

Further activities

- Design and produce a leaflet describing the best features of your model home.
- Design and make a model garden to go with your home.
- Design and make a plan of a town of the future.
- Design and make clothes of the future.
- Design a model car of the future.

Badges

Starting points
- Collect and discuss different kinds of badges.
- Investigate symbols and logos, eg road signs, sports club badges, company logos.
- Survey the main interests and hobbies of the children in the class.

Materials
Card of various kinds, graphic materials, paper fasteners, safety pins, adhesive tape, glue, fabrics (eg cotton, felt squares), fabric printing inks and materials, material for decoration, rulers, LOGO computer program.

Teaching notes

Badges originally came from coats of arms which were used to decorate and identify knights in jousting tournaments. Knights chose their own symbols, eg crosses for faith, lions for strength and so on. (What might other animals stand for?) By the late Middle Ages there were rigid conventions about lines used in heraldic badges. Each line was named: (see diagram). Invite children to reproduce these using LOGO.

By the late Middle Ages line conventions were used in heraldic badges; each line was named, eg:

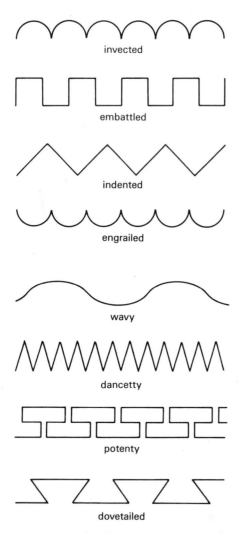

invected

embattled

indented

engrailed

wavy

dancetty

potenty

dovetailed

Invite the children to reproduce these using LOGO

Discuss ways of making the badge designs more interesting through use of unusual shapes or by including moving parts, eg a waving hand or a flap which opens. Show children how symbols are used to represent ideas on signs and in logos. Encourage them to observe and analyse how symbols convey meaning without the use of words. Explore examples of symbols that could represent hobbies or pastimes, eg reading (an opening book?). Children should draw and experiment with several designs before deciding to make their prototype badge.

Key questions could include:
- Who wears badges? What badges do they wear?
- Why do people wear badges? What do badges tell us?
- What would you like your badge to show?
- How could you make your badge design interesting and unusual?

Fabric badges can be made using simple fabric printing (see Techniques pp53 and 57). These can be sewn onto T-shirts or sports kits, if desired.

Extension activities
- Display badges and discuss the design effectiveness.
- Hold a quiz. From picture clues what common symbols and logos can children recognise? (Try contacting The Royal College of Arms for further information.)
- Organise a badge bazaar, swap-shop, or charity event.
- Design name badges for children to wear, eg to help visitors or for use on visits.
- Design and make relief card badges to serve as printing blocks.

Related investigations
CLOTHES theme: *Book 1* Hats p12, Safety first p14; *Book 2* Toy clothes p12, Spectacles p14; *Book 3* Sports kit p14; *Book 4* Designer shoes p12, Fancy dress show p14. See also: *Book 1* School signs p38.

Badges

Challenge

Can you design and make your own badge to show what your main interest or hobby is, or to show what school or club you belong to?

Design proposal

- Should your badge be clear and easily seen from a distance?
- How will you show what your badge means without using words?
- Draw ideas for badges, using your own symbols or logo.
- How will you make your badge interesting?
- Could it have a moving part?

Evaluating

- Can other people see clearly what your badge is showing?
- Is your badge well made?
- Is it easy to fix on clothes? Does it stay on?
- Is your badge interesting to look at?
- Are you pleased with your badge? What do other people think?

Planning and making

- Think what shape your badge might be (it does not have to be round).
- What materials do you need to make your badge?
- What size will look best for your badge (try different sizes)?
- How will you decorate your badge?
- How will you fix your badge to clothes?

Further activities

- Display a collection of badges. Which are well made? Which have best designs?
- Collect pictures of different badges, symbols and logos. Which of these can others recognise?
- Study the Highway Code. Which signs and symbols can you recognise?
- Design a badge or logo for a sweat shirt. Make a motto to go with your badge.

Sports kit

Starting points
- Discuss and show examples of different types and styles of sports kit.
- Collect illustations of sports kit showing design elements, eg flashings, badges, and trims.
- Invite a local sports team representative to discuss choice and care of kit.

Materials
Graphic materials, figure templates, various cloth materials, old sheets, fabric crayons, printing materials, tie and dye equipment, pva adhesive, needles and thread.

Teaching notes
Investigate current sports kit for design and quality, eg type of material, strength of seams and so on. Consult catalogues and magazines for clothes patterns and commercial examples of sportswear. Children could write to other schools or clubs for information about colours, styles and kit. Discuss the use of sponsorship in sport (who might sponsor your team?) and the use of logos, badges, flashings and trims. Brainstorm criteria by which sports kits could be judged. Elements to consider include visibility, strength of material, washability.

Key questions could include:
- Why do people wear special kit for different sports?
- What different sports kits are there?
- What is your favourite design of sports kit?
- What materials is it made from?
- How could the quality of materials used be important for a sports kit?

Children could conduct a market survey to find out the most popular colours and designs for sports kits. Techniques particularly suitable for design work include fabric crayons, simple needlework, fabric printing and tie and dye (see Techniques pp53, 56, 57 and 61).

Extension activities
- Design and make a bag to hold the sports kit.
- Design other kinds of kit, eg swimming, art aprons/shirts, first-aid.
- Design a badge for the kit (see p12).
- Design a school uniform for children, or for teachers!
- Design and make an item of clothing for others, eg a bobble hat or scarf in school colours (a leaving present for someone?).

Related investigations
CLOTHES theme: *Book 1* Hats p12, Safety first p14; *Book 2* Toy clothes p12, Spectacles p14; *Book 3* Badges p12; *Book 4* Designer shoes p12, Fancy dress show p14.

Sports kit

Challenge

Can you design a new sports kit for your school or club? Can you make a small-scale model of your sports kit design?

Design proposal

- What sport will you design your kit for?
- Will the colours need to be different for other teams or players?
- What will make your kit clearly seen by other players and spectators?
- Will it need to include patterns, a badge or trimming?
- Draw or sketch your ideas.

Planning and making

- Choose your best design for a new sports kit.
- Can you make a small-scale model of your sports kit?
- What materials will you need?
- How will you join the materials?
- Do you need to colour or decorate the material? If so, how?

Evaluating

- What do you think of your design for a new sports kit?
- How does your kit compare with other designs for sports kits?
- How is your kit different from other kits?
- Is it made of good material, hard-wearing and easy to clean?
- What do other people think of your new sports kit?

Further activities

- Can you design a bag for the kit?
- Can you help make sure the kit will not get lost?
- Can you design a kit for another sport or activity?
- Can you make a model of your design?
- Can you find out what other people's favourite sports kit designs are?

Broadcasting

Starting points

- Survey children's favourite TV and radio programmes.
- Analyse the content of TV and radio programmes in the Radio Times or other listings magazines.
- Tape small sections of children's TV and radio programmes (eg Newsround, Blue Peter, Radio 5) for children to comment upon critically.

Materials

Video camera, video recorder, cassette recorder, microphone, graphic materials.

Teaching notes

Borrow a video camera from a local teachers'/curriculum centre or parent. If you cannot get a camera, concentrate on making a radio programme. Alternatively, broadcast 'live' in a school assembly.

Key questions could include:
- What programmes would people be interested in watching? (Consider the audience for the broadcast.)
- What programmes realistically could be made? Consider:
  - a magazine style programme focussing on current school issues
  - a roving reporter asking children in the school about topics of interest (eg describe your worst and best moments at the school)
  - an interview with a prominent person in the school.
  - a quiz programme
  - filming a performance written and produced by the children
  - a factual programme (eg 'How to use the school library', ideas for making things, an art gallery showing children's work, a visitor's guide to the school)
  - advertisements for products, events, the school.
- What elements will enliven the broadcast? (Advertising, jingles, theme tunes.)
- How will the broadcast be made as interesting as possible? (Editing, need for performances to be well rehearsed, excellence in writing scripts.) These tasks could be shared between members of a group.

A word processor will assist in the writing and editing of scripts.

Consider using this activity towards the end of the school year to give children the necessary time to prepare and produce the programme. Encourage the children to reflect back on their achievements in the school year and include these in the broadcast. See also *Recording Achievement in Primary Schools* by R. Fisher (Simon & Schuster Education).

Extension activities

- Produce a programme that will interest very small children.
- Tape a favourite short book or story (with sound effects) for someone else to listen to.
- Investigate the history of broadcasting and how it has changed over the years.
- Interview parents and members of the local community about their favourite TV and radio programmes from the past.

Related investigations

COMMUNICATION theme: *Book 1* Greeting card p16, Telephone p18; *Book 2* Stamps p16, Make a code p18; *Book 3* Making books p18; *Book 4* Envelope factory p16, Newspapers p18.

Broadcasting

Challenge

Can you produce your own television or radio programme of class news, events and children's interests?

Design proposal

- What items will you include in your programme? Consider:
  - reporting on school events
  - news from home
  - an entertaining performance, sketch or short play
  - music.
- How long will the programme be?
- Will your programme need a theme tune?
- Who will be asked to watch the programme?

Evaluating

- Did you produce your own TV or radio programme?
- Ask other people if they liked your broadcast.
- Could you have presented your broadcast in any other way?
- Could you have improved your broadcast?

Planning and making

- Will your broadcast be made using a tape recorder, video recorder or by other means?
- What jobs will different children need to do?
- Will you need to make any signs or pictures for different items?
- Will you need to write a script for the items in your broadcast?

Further activities

- Create an advert for your broadcast.
- Carry out a survey to find out children's favourite TV or radio programmes.
- Make a programme that young children will learn from and enjoy.
- Tape record a piece of music that children in your class have written and performed.

Making books

Starting points
- Encourage the children to bring in a collection of their favourite books.
- Discuss books from different times and cultures in terms of their content and aesthetic appeal (with respect to bookmaking as a craft).
- Set up a display of books in the book corner for children to handle, read and discuss.

Materials ▲
Graphic materials, cold water paste, brushes, needles, thread, printing equipment and inks, craft knives, cutting mats, plain fabrics, fabric inks, potatoes, fabric crayons, fabric glue, wax crayons, furniture polish (spray type), cardboard, hardboard, masking tape, bookbinding tape.

Teaching notes

Techniques
Begin with simple books made from paper and card and then progressively refine skills through the use of a variety of materials. Great emphasis should be placed upon care in measuring, cutting and finishing to produce work of quality.

Extension activities
- Design and make a small display stand for a book.
- Study the history of the development of writing.
- Challenge children to redesign the reading corner to show their own and published books to best advantage.

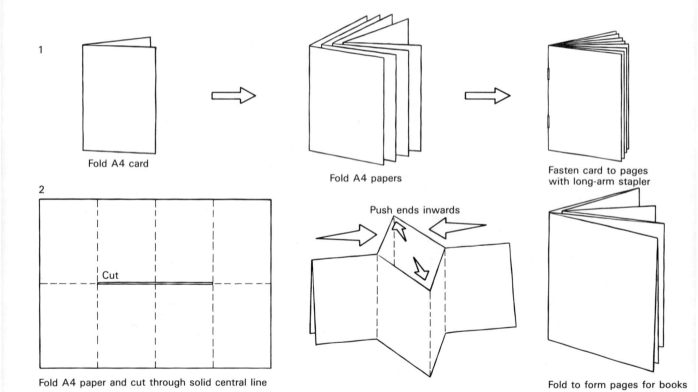

1
Fold A4 card

Fold A4 papers

Fasten card to pages with long-arm stapler

2
Fold A4 paper and cut through solid central line

Cut

Push ends inwards

Fold to form pages for books

For more advanced books, see Techniques p48. Encourage the children to design and make their own book covers, end papers and fly leaves through techniques such as marbling, fabric printing, printing and stencilling, and tie and dye (see Techniques pp53, 57, 59, and 61).

Related investigations
COMMUNICATION theme: *Book 1* Greeting card p16, Telephone p18; *Book 2* Stamps p16, Make a code p18; *Book 3* Broadcasting p16; *Book 4* Envelope factory p16, Newspapers p18.

Making books

Challenge

Can you design and make a book for a favourite story or interest of yours?

Design proposal

- What kind of book could you design?
- For whom is your book?
- What will be the shape and size of your book?
- How many pages will your book have?
- Draw ideas for your book design.

Planning and making

- What type of paper will you use for your book?
- How will you make the cover of your book?
- How will you join the pages to the cover?
- What material will you use for binding your book?
- How will you decorate the cover of your book?

Evaluating

- Did you design and make your own book?
- Ask other people what they think about your book.
- Is your book well made?
- Are the contents interesting and well presented?
- Is the cover well designed?
- Could your book be improved?

Further activities

- Design and make a book-jacket to protect your book.
- Design and make a poster to advertise your book.
- Write a review of your own or someone else's book.
- Design and make a bookmark showing something about your book.
- Can you make a series of books based upon a particular theme or character?
- Design and make a pop-up book to surprise a friend.

Bird scarer

Starting points
- Discuss the need to protect seeds and young plants from birds and other pests.
- Find out what bird scarers or scarecrows the children may have seen.
- Display reference, story and poetry books about birds.

Materials ▲
Card of various kinds, string, wire coathangers, lengths of wood, foil, plastic bags and bottles, corks, polystyrene, bottle tops, tins, paper fasteners.

Teaching notes
Seeds are a good source of protein if eaten by birds or other animals (like us!). Farmers and gardeners can lose a lot of the seed they sow to birds. Birds and insects that eat seeds and prevent food plants like corn, fruit or vegetables from growing are pests. We need to scare pests away. Bird scarers may be needed to keep birds away while the seed is germinating, but they must not be cruel or hurt the birds. They must also be made of weatherproof materials.

Key questions could include:
- What may frighten birds away? (Movement, noise, shapes?)
- What noises frighten birds? How can they be made?
- What shapes frighten birds? Why?
- How can you make something outside move? Rotate? Swing? Twist?
- What weather-proof materials could a bird scarer be made from?

The following are some techniques that may help in making a bird scarer:

Extension activities
- Create a 3-D frieze incorporating birds (mobile?) and pest scarer or scarecrow.
- Get the children to research into birds using reference and study material (send off to the RSPB for resources list).
- Investigate ways of protecting plants from other pests.
- Invite a farmer or market gardener to discuss pests or be interviewed about them.
- Create a simple food chain to show the inter-dependence of life.
- Write to aid agencies for information on the causes of famine in the developing world. Can we devise a system that might help?
- Study other pests, eg insects (fleas can go without food for 1½ years; at a single meal an adult flea consumes its own weight in blood). Are there any human pests?

Related investigations
CONSERVATION theme: *Book 1* Amazing monsters p20, Minbeast trap p22; *Book 2* Pet home p20, Weather station p22; *Book 3* Plant waterer p22; *Book 4* Bird table p20, Conservation area p22. See also: *Book 4* Down on the farm p10.

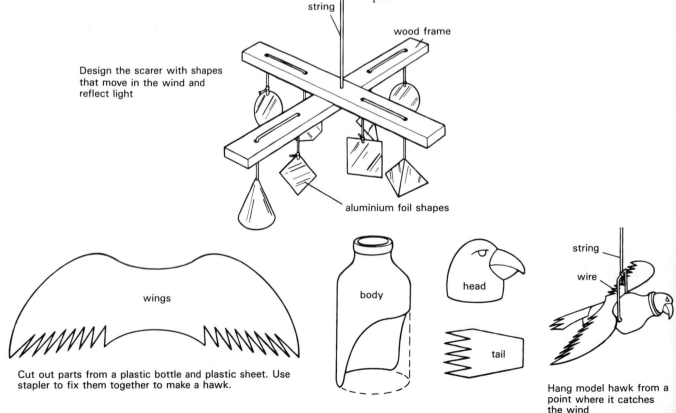

string

wood frame

Design the scarer with shapes that move in the wind and reflect light

aluminium foil shapes

wings

Cut out parts from a plastic bottle and plastic sheet. Use stapler to fix them together to make a hawk.

body

head

tail

string

wire

Hang model hawk from a point where it catches the wind

Bird scarer

Challenge

Birds love to eat new seeds in the fields and fruit growing in gardens and allotments. Can you design and make a bird scarer to keep the birds away?

Design proposal

- What sort of thing would frighten birds away?
- Should your bird scarer move?
- Should it make a noise?
- Should it look like something that would frighten birds?
- How will your bird scarer be held in place on a windy day?
- Draw ideas of what your bird scarer might look like.

Evaluating

- Have you designed and made a bird scarer?
- Will your bird scarer keep birds away? How could you test this?
- Is your bird scarer weather-proof? Will it stand up to wind and rain?
- Is your bird scarer a good design? What do other people think?
- How could your bird scarer be improved?

Planning and making

- What materials will you need to make your bird scarer? Remember, they must be weather-proof.
- What tools will you need?
- Will you need other people to help?
- Safety! Take care when you are making your bird scarer.
- You must not hurt the birds, so avoid sharp edges on your scarer.

Further activities

- Find out more about your favourite birds from bird books.
- Find out what other pests there are in the garden. How might plants be protected from them?
- Show others how your bird scarer works.
- Find out what a pesticide is. Why are pesticides dangerous?
- Write a poem or story about a scarecrow.

Plant waterer

Starting points
- Discuss what happens when plants are left unwatered, eg during holidays.
- Show and discuss examples of withered, surviving and thriving plants. Carry out scientific tests on these.
- Collect and display pictures and information on different types of indoor plant.

Materials ▲
Plastic bags and pots, glass jars and containers, string, elastic bands, Plasticine, wire, lengths of wood, card, plant pots and pot plants, sponge, blotting paper, bulldog clips, plastic tubing.

Teaching notes
Discuss and investigate what plants need to live, how the needs of different plants vary, and how important it is to take care of the natural world (even indoors). Show how plants can be propagated, and the wide variety that grows from seeds, eg fruit pips or stones, and from cuttings. But all need water.

Key questions could include:
- How much water does a plant need to live? (Estimate, then test.)
- How often should a plant be watered? (The needs of plants vary.)
- Are there some plants that need no water? (All plants need *some* water.)
- What are different ways to water plants? (From above or below, with a hose, can, by rain and so on.)
- What problems are there in keeping plants watered? (Holidays?)

The problem of watering plants can be tackled in different ways (see diagrams). The children may need to be given clues to techniques that may help to solve the problem.

Extension activities
- Display and compare the efficiency of different plant waterers.
- Estimate how much water a plant needs in a day, a week, a month, a year, for the life of the plant (compare with a human?).
- Discuss the problems of drought, starvation and crop failure in different parts of the world (send for information from aid agencies).
- Invite a horticulturalist or market gardener to discuss problems and solutions when watering and caring for plants.
- Grow and market (for a good cause) your own pot plant propagations, using your own plant waterers (create an advert and advice booklet for this).

Related investigations
CONSERVATION theme: *Book 1* Amazing monsters p20, Minibeast trap p22; *Book 2* Pet home p20, Weather station p22; *Book 3* Bird scarer p20; *Book 4* Bird table p20, Conservation area p22. See also: *Book 1* School stall p46; *Book 4* Down on the farm p10.

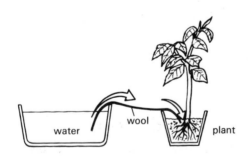

water   wool   plant

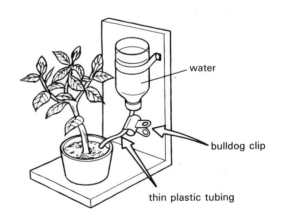

water

bulldog clip

thin plastic tubing

Plant waterer

Challenge

We need to water our plants when we are away for the weekend or on holiday. Can you design and make a plant waterer that will slowly water the plants while you are away?

Design proposal

- Discuss and decide how much water your pot plant needs.
- Can you design a container that will give water over a long time to your plant?
- Will you water the plant from
  - underneath?
  - above?
- How will you fix your plant waterer securely in place?
- Draw you ideas for a plant waterer.

Planning and making

- Will your plant waterer give enough water to keep the plant healthy?
- What materials will you need to make the waterer?
- How will you fix your water so it does not leak or spill any water?
- How will you test your waterer to see if it works?
- Where will be the best place to put the plant so that it will not need a lot of water?

Evaluating

- Have you designed and made a plant waterer?
- Does your plant waterer do its job?
- Have you tested it?
- What do other people think of it?
- Could you improve it?

Further activities

- Can you change your waterer to water many plants at one time?
- Experiment by giving the same kind of plant a little water, a lot of water and no water. What do you find out?
- Investigate if it matters whether you water plants on the leaves, at the stem or round the edge.
- Design and make your own pot for a pot plant.
- Write and illustrate your own book of advice for caring for pot plants (advertise your plant waterer in it).

Lunch box

Starting points
- Read *The Lighthouse Keeper's Lunch* by R. and D. Armitage (Puffin) for a context setting. The lighthouse keeper's lunch is being eaten by birds as it is winched to the lighthouse. Can you make a secure lunch box to protect the food from the birds?
- Survey what children have in their packed lunch boxes. Chart findings.
- Investigate lunch box containers. Compare design, capacity, durability and cost.

Materials ▲
Card of various kinds, graphic materials, card-cutting tools.

Teaching notes
Discuss with children the criteria by which a lunch box might be judged, for example:
- Convenience of shape, storage and handling.
- Durability and strength to withstand rough treatment.
- Capacity to hold necessary food and drink.
- Exterior design, colour and decoration of cover.
- Interior design; compartments and need to wrap each food separately.
- Cost to buy.

What order of priority would children rank such criteria in judging a lunch box?

Key questions could include:
- What is the best way to protect a packed lunch for school?
- What do you think of the design of lunch boxes (show different examples)?
- What is the best way of keeping lunch boxes in school?
- Who packs your lunch box?
- Are your packed lunches healthy? In what ways?

Explain that when designers are creating something, they either design something new, or they take an old design and try to improve on it. Which will the children try to do? It may be helpful to provide some flat-pack nets to be assembled by the children to help them generate their own ideas (see diagram). One of the constraints of the design proposal is that their lunch boxes should have compartments. What different compartments do they need? One way of making compartments is by interlocking card (see diagram).

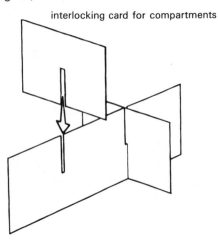

interlocking card for compartments

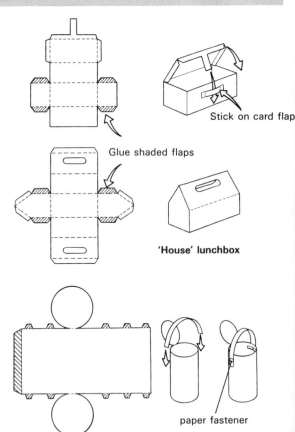

Stick on card flap

Glue shaded flaps

'House' lunchbox

paper fastener

Extension activities
- Design a cover for your lunch box based on a theme, eg healthy eating.
- Study insulation materials that would help keep food cool in a lunch box.
- Help solve storage problems in school by designing and making a model trolley for storing and moving lunch boxes.
- Study healthy choices for lunch boxes. Purchase a variety of foods suitable for a packed lunch, eg breads, spreads, meats, cheeses, fish, fruit, salad. Ask children to choose a filling and to make a packed lunch sandwich (paying for food at cost).
- Make a poster or advert for healthy eating, your own sandwich recipe or your lunch box.

Related investigations
FOOD theme: *Book 1* Bread p24, Cookies p26; *Book 2* Breakfast table p24, Picnic time p26; *Book 3* Tea party p26; *Book 4* Tasty salads p24, School dinners p26. See also *Book 1* Lighthouse p10.

Lunch box

Challenge

Packed lunches can easily get squashed and damaged. Can you design and make a lunch box to hold and protect your packed lunch?

Design proposal

- What is the best kind of design for a lunch box?
- Are you going to design a new lunch box, or adapt an old one?
- Your lunch box should contain different compartments for the different foods, drinks and utensils you need.
- Draw your ideas for the different compartments in a lunch box.

Planning and making

- What different foods and drink are going into your lunch box?
- Will your lunch box design hold this food and drink?
- Make a model of your lunch box.
- What materials will you need?
- When you have made your lunch box model, design your own label for it (the label should carry a message).

Evaluating

- Have you designed a lunch box for a packed lunch?
- Have you made a model of your lunch box design?
- Have you designed a label for it?
- How could your lunch box be improved?
- What do other people think of it?

Further activities

- Compare your lunch box model with others.
- Design a way of keeping things cool in your lunch box.
- Design a model trolley for storing and moving lunch boxes.
- Work out recipes for a different packed lunch for each day of the school week.
- Design a poster to encourage children to eat healthy foods for lunch.

Tea party

Starting points
- Read the story of the Mad Hatter's Tea Party from *Alice in Wonderland* by Lewis Carroll.
- Brainstorm what you need to think about when planning a party.
- Discuss possible themes and reasons for a tea party, eg an approaching festival or celebration, an invitation to local old folks, community helpers or school visitors.

Materials ▲
Graphic and printing materials, card, cardboard, card-cutting equipment.

Teaching notes

Try to relate this activity to a real event such as an end-of-term party, festival or celebration. The theme of the party could relate to other school work, such as history project (a historical party in costume?), or a social occasion after a school event such as a concert. The theme of the party could be used to inform work on the food used or designs for partywear, particularly if it relates to a multi-cultural festival, eg Chinese motifs for Chinese New Year, Rangoli patterns for Diwali, Islamic patterns for Eid (the end of Ramadan), Easter or Christmas motifs.

Key questions could include:
- What reason could we have for organising a tea party in school?
- Who could we invite? How will we invite them?
- Where could we have it? What place would be best?
- When should it be? What would be the best time? For how long?
- What else do we need to think about when planning a party?

Things to think about could include making an invitation list and designing invitation cards, planning a menu of food and drink, designing place settings, place names and place mats, and making party hats or clothes. Plan the preparations and clearing up afterwards! As part of the preparations, children might like to make a party hat for a friend (can they make the hat reflect their friend's personality and interests?). For techniques that might be useful see pp56, 57, 58 and 59.

Extension activities
- Children could act or write their own version of the Mad Hatter's Tea Party.
- Design decorations for place settings, eg doilies cut to their own design, paper plate or cup designs, serviette origami and woven place mats.
- Create a party dish recipe, eg biscuits (see *Book 1* p26).
- Design a party hat (see *Book 1* p12) and party clothes (see *Book 4* p14).
- Calculate the cost of the party and per person costs. How can we fund the party?

Related investigatons
FOOD theme: *Book 1* Bread p24, Cookies p26; *Book 2* Breakfast table p24, Picnic time p26; *Book 3* Lunch box p24; *Book 4* Tasty salads p24, School dinners p26. See also: *Book 1* Hats p12; *Book 4* Fancy dress show p14.

Tea party

Challenge

Can you plan and organise a tea party on a theme of your own choice?

Design proposal

- What kind of theme could your tea party have:
  - a birthday party?
  - a dressing-up party?
  - a special celebration?
- Who would you invite to the party?
- What menu of food and drink would you have?
- What might you need to design for the party:
  - party invitations?
  - party hats?
- Draw or write your ideas for a tea party.

Planning and making

- Have you got ideas for your tea party?
- Have you chosen a theme for the tea party?
- Have you designed and made invitation cards?
- What will you eat and drink? Have you planned a menu?
- What materials do you need for your party?
- How will you organise your tea party? Do a plan for it.

Evaluating

- Have you planned your tea party?
- Did you choose a good theme for your party?
- Was your party well planned?
- How could you have improved your party plans?
- What did others think of the tea party?

Further activities

- Can you design and make some decorations for your tea party?
- Can you design table settings and place name cards?
- Can you create your own party dish recipe?
- Can you design your special party hat or clothes?
- Can you work out how much your tea party will cost? Who will pay?

Design a room

Starting points
- Make a survey of the rooms children have in their homes.
- Ask them to do a floor plan of the rooms in their houses.
- Tell them to close their eyes and take themselves on a 'mind's eye' journey through a real or imaginary house. Ask them to write or describe what they 'saw' or imagined in the house.

Materials ▲
Various cardboard boxes, (eg shoe boxes), card, fabrics, graphic and printing materials, tie and dye materials, plastic sheets (optional).

Teaching notes

In this task the children are asked to be architects and interior designers. Do they know what jobs such people do? The aim is to create mini-environments of their own choosing and design. This work can be undertaken individually, in pairs or small groups. Stimulus can be provided by reading to the children examples of fictional rooms such as the burrow of Bilbo in *The Hobbit*, or *Stig of the Dump's* hide-out.

Key questions could include:
- What is your favourite room?
- What is special about it?
- If you could have any kind of bedroom, what would it be like?
- Imagine you had a hide-out all of your own. Where would it be? What would it be like?

Ask children to consider and discuss what factors they need to consider in designing a model room, eg shape of room, position of door(s), window(s), floor and wall coverings, furniture and any special objects. They will need to think how others can see into their model rooms, eg from above (looking down into a box) or from one side (into an enclosed box, perhaps with a hinged wall like a doll's house). For ideas that may be helpful in modelling the rooms and furniture see Techniques pp50 and 53.

Extension activities
- Children may like to put toy figures in their rooms, but it is better if they can model these for themselves, eg from pipe cleaners or modelling materials.
- Ask children to design the building environment of their model room, showing how it relates to its surroundings.
- Challenge the children to find ten or more mathmatical facts about their model, eg shape, measurement, and number data.
- Use the model room as a stimulus for creative writing, eg what dramatic conversation or quarrel or news story could have taken place there?
- Invite an architect or interior designer to talk about his or her work and predict future trends. Ask children to respond with their own interior designs for the future.

Related investigations
HOME theme: *Book 1* Photograph frame p28, Milk today p30; *Book 2* Book ends p28, Gift wrapping p30; *Book 3* Candle holder p30; *Book 4* Mobile for baby p28, Burglar alarm p30. See also: *Book 3* Home of the future p10.

Design a room

Challenge
Can you design and make a model of a room of your own?

Design proposal
- What kind of room could you design?
- You can choose any kind or room:
  - a bedroom
  - bathroom
  - kitchen
  - living room or any other room.
- Your room could be part of any human home:
  - a house
  - a caravan
  - a treehouse
  - a boat
  - a spaceship or whatever.
- It can be from any time – past, present or future.
- What designs can you draw for your room?

Planning and making
- Have you drawn the room you will make?
- Have you shown what kind of furniture it contains and how it is decorated?
- What materials will you need to make your model room?
- How will people see into your model room?
- How will you decorate your room?

Evaluating
- Have you designed and made a model room?
- Have you shown its furniture and decoration?
- Is it well designed?
- Is it well made?
- What do other people think of your room?

Further activities
- Create model people to go in your model room.
- Design a house or building to go with your model room.
- Can you find ten or more different things to write or say about your room?
- Can you write a poem, play or story set in your room?
- Can you design and make a room of the future?

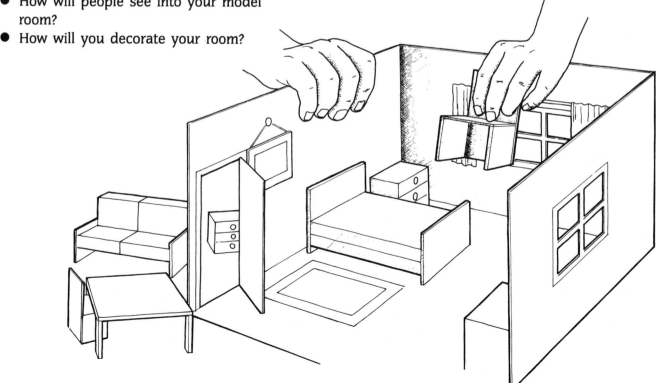

Candle holder

Starting points
- Collect and discuss examples of different kinds of candle holder (real or pictorial).
- Discuss when candles are used today (at home, festivals and celebrations).
- Collect and display a variety of candles.

Materials ▲
Candles, candle-making materials (optional), graphic and modelling materials (eg clay, Plasticine), card, adhesive.

Teaching notes
Encourage the children to find a purpose for making candles. Candle holders may make useful presents and may form part of preparations for a festival or celebration, eg *Christian*; St. Lucia's Day, Christmas, Candlemas, Easter (Paschal Candle) *Jewish*; Chanukkah, the Menorah and candles lit each Sabbath *Hindu/Sikh*; Diwali (festival of lights).

Discuss how all homes were candle-lit or lit by oil lamps in the past. Ask what would happen today at home if there was a power cut.

Key questions could include:
- Do you ever light candles at home?
- When do you light them?
- What do you have at home that will hold candles?
- What are candles made from?
- How are thay made?

The following are some techniques which may help in making candle holders (see also clay techniques p52):

Extension activities
- Design and make a box in which to store or present your candle holder. Illustrate the lid of your box with a picture of your candle holder.
- How would you persuade others to buy your candle holder? Design an advert to tell others about your candle holder, or a set of instructions on how to make one.
- Cost the raw materials, and ask the children to work out the cost of their models.
- Challenge them to make a Menorah, candelabra or multi-branched candle holder.
- Examine different types of candles; ask children to devise fair tests to find the best value for money. Could they make their own cheaper or better candles?

Related investigations
HOME theme: *Book 1* Photograph frame p28, Milk today p30; *Book 2* Book-ends p28, Gift wrapping p30; *Book 3* Design a room p28; *Book 4* Mobile for baby p28, Burglar alarm p30.

Roll clay into ball

Rotate pot, gently squeezing from inside to make indentations with thumbs

Decorate using clay tools; glaze and fire

For further work with clay, see p52

Candle holder

Challenge

Can you make a candle holder to hold one or more candles for a special occasion?

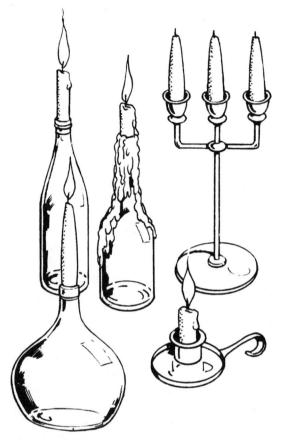

Design proposal

- What might your candle holder look like?
- Will your candle holder hold one or more candles?
- Can you design a candle holder that will:
  - hold candles upright?
  - hold candles firmly?
  - be difficult to knock over?
  - be interesting and attractive?
- Draw your ideas for designing and decorating your candle holder.
- What you will do with your candle holder once you have made it?

Planning and making

- Have you thought of a design for your candle holder?
- What materials will you need?
- DANGER! Your candle holder must be made of materials that will not easily burn.
- How many candles will it hold?
- How will you decorate your candle holder?

Evaluating

- Have you designed and made a candle holder?
- Does it hold one or more candles firmly in place?
- Is it made of safe materials and difficult to knock over?
- Is it well designed and decorated?
- What do other people think of your candle holder?

Further activities

- Can you make a box in which to put your candle holder?
- Can you create an advert for your candle holder?
- Can you design a candle holder that will hold a lot of candles?
- Can you work out how much it cost to make your candle holder?
- How can you test to find out which candles are the best value for money?

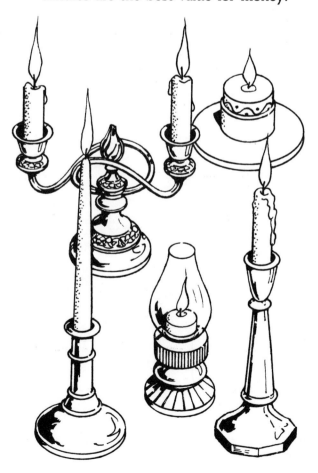

Wheel of chance

Starting points

- Collect and discuss a variety of rotating mechanisms and wheels.
- Compare and contrast examples of rotation, eg bicycle wheels, clocks, record players, display stands, fairground wheels, roundabouts, the Earth and Moon.
- Investigate probability via games and materials with random numbers, eg dice, spinners, cards, tossing coins, choosing lots, and the chances they offer.

Materials ▲

Card, wood dowelling, cutting tools, junk materials, construction kits, pencils.

Teaching notes

A wheel of chance can be made in different ways, for example:

- With a spinning arrow pointer.
- With a spinning wheel of numbers and fixed pointer.
- With a spinning top.

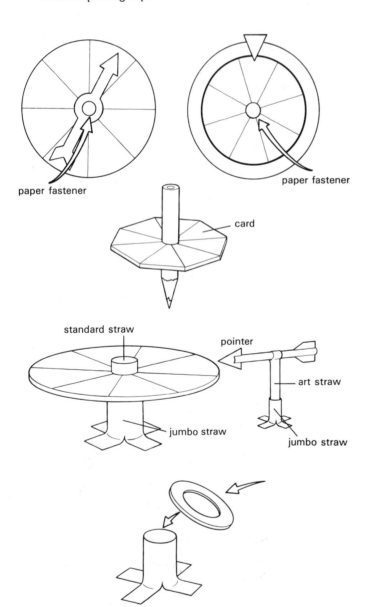

paper fastener

paper fastener

card

standard straw

pointer

art straw

jumbo straw

jumbo straw

the same idea can be used for 'toss the plastic washer' game

Experiment with different diameters of card and lengths of spindle. Encourage the exploration of different ideas using the materials available.

Key questions could include:

- How can you make a wheel spin round?
- What could hold the wheel in position?
- How could you decorate or design the wheel?
- What numbers, words or symbols would you use for decoration?
- What chances would you offer of winning?

The wheel of chance might involve numbers or words, eg names (of horses, children), letters, symbols or colours. The wheel must, of course, offer fair chances for all. Discuss the uses to which a wheel of chance could be put, eg for fun or to raise money. Obviously it presents many opportunities to explore concepts of probability related to maths ATs.

Extension activities

- Ask the children to create a game using the wheel of chance, write rules and test.
- Investigate whether a wheel of chance gives even chances under test conditions.
- Create an advert or poster for a wheel of chance.
- Plan a fund-raising event using a wheel of chance.
- Design and make a model using the principle of a rotating wheel, eg fairground wheel, roundabout, display stand etc. Could a power source drive the wheel? For ideas see *Book 3* Windmill p46 and *Book 4* Water mill p46.

Related investigations

RECREATION theme: *Book 1* Jigsaw p32, Fishing game p34; *Book 2* Baby toy p32, Climbing frame p34; *Book 3* Board game p34; *Book 4* Making puppets p32, Performing a puppet play p34. See also: *Book 2* Spinner p42; *Book 3* Playground p38, Windmill p46; *Book 4* Water mill p46.

Wheel of chance

Challenge

Can you design and make a wheel of chance game?

Design proposal

- Can you design a wheel of chance game which:
  - has numbers or other symbols marked on a wheel-shaped piece of card?
  - can spin round and stop anywhere by chance?
  - can be used to find a winner?
- Can you make a wheel of chance that is:
  - strong and secure?
  - safe to use?
- How will you design your wheel? Draw your ideas.

Evaluating

- Have you designed and made a wheel of chance?
- Does it rotate smoothly?
- Is it well made and safe to use?
- Does it give fair chances of winning?
- Could it be improved? What do other people think?

Planning and making

- Have you drawn your chosen design?
- How will the wheel of chance rotate?
- What materials will you need?
- How will your wheel of chance be held in place?
- How will you decorate your wheel?

Further activities

- Can you make up a game using a spinning top or wheel?
- Design and make a poster to advertise your spinning wheel game.
- Show other people how you designed, made and tested your wheel of chance.
- Can you design and make another model that rotates, such as a roundabout?

Board game

Teaching notes

This activity is best undertaken by pairs or small groups. A story book can be a useful stimulus. The story book starter could be a class reading book or one of the children's choice. Other game ideas could be developed from a class topic or theme from history, geography or science. Discuss links with mathematical concepts such as shape, tesselation and number. Links with language work include writing rules and instructions.

Key questions could include:
- Will your game be one of luck or skill, or both?
- How many players do you want in your game?
- What sort of board could you have?
- What could you use to make the players' pieces?
- How will the winner be decided? By the first to reach a particular place, the one with the most points, cards or tokens, or in some other way?

If dice are needed, encourage children to make their own (or a spinner), and their own pieces rather than use ready-made counters. Also encourage them to make a box for their pieces, as these are easily lost or broken! Simple fabric bags can be made to hold the pieces.

Simple board designs are usually more effective, so that rules can be easily followed. A symmetrical game will lend itself to printing techniques, eg a draughts-type game could be designed using potato prints. The same print block can be used for alternating colours (see Techniques p58). Such a board could form the basis for a variety of games, eg a race game or paying forfeits when landing on different colours. Consider fabric as well as card for boards.

Extension activities
- Work out how much it costs to make your game.
- Design and make a suitable container to store all parts of the game.
- Try out the game on others, record results and modify if necessary.
- Invent other types of game: a maze game, a word game, a calculator game, a Trivial Pursuit quiz-type game based on a class topic, a game for PE, a game for teaching younger children, eg a matching game, or adapt a commercial or TV game.
- Ask children to work out and write down the best strategy for winning their own game or a commonly played game such as noughts and crosses.

Related investigations

RECREATION theme: *Book 1* Jigsaw p32, Fishing game p34; *Book 2* Baby toy p32, Climbing frame p34; *Book 3* Wheel of chance p32; *Book 4* Making puppets p32, Performing a puppet play p34.

Board game

Challenge

Board games are expensive. Save money and make your own! Can you design and make your own board game?

Design proposal

- Think about the different kinds of board game there are.
- Why not make up a board game based on a story that you know? You could use the characters, setting or events for your game.
- What will be the aim of your game?
- How will players move across the board?
- How many players? How many pieces? What rules?
- Write or draw your board game ideas.

Evaluating

- Have you designed and made a board game?
- Have you tested out the game with your friends?
- Did they understand the rules?
- Did they like your game?
- How could it be improved?

Planning and making

- Have you some ideas for your board game?
- What materials will you need to make your game?
- Will you need to make a dice or spinner for the game?
- How will you decorate your board?
- Make your board and rules as clear and simple as possible.

Further activities

- Can you make a box or container to keep your game in?
- Can you make a poster or advert for your game?
- Try your game on others and record the results.
- Can you make a game that will teach something to younger children?
- Can you make a game using a calculator or computer?

Litter bin

Starting points
- Conduct a survey of kinds of litter in the school grounds or local area (children should wear protective gloves when collecting litter).
- On the survey record the design and location of litter bins.
- Discuss the design of different types of litter bins and recycling containers.

Materials ▲
Graphic materials, junk materials, card, cardboard, craft knives, metal rule, cutting mat, square cm wood, hacksaws, bench hooks, polythene (carrier bags, bin bags), protective gloves.

Teaching notes
The survey of litter should reveal what kinds of litter will need to be dealt with. This will be a guide to the shape and size of the bin.

Key questions could include:
- Will one type of litter bin accommodate the variety of litter collected? (Need for variety of types and sizes of bin.)
- How will animals at night be deterred from entering or upsetting the bin? (Need for stability, inclusion of lid.)
- What differences should there be between litter bins inside and outside the school building? (Weather-proofing, protection from animals.)

Techniques
- Make prototypes from card. Investigate how they can be weather-proofed. Full-sized bins could be made from cardboard (see Techniques p50) and weather-proofed using polythene.

Extension activities
- Test out a variety of locations for bins to see where the most litter is collected.
- Graphical work on types of litter collected.
- Investigate what happens to waste food from the school dining room.
- Study a variety of recycled materials. What they can be used for?

Related investigations
SCHOOL theme: *Book 1* Musical instruments p36, School signs p38; *Book 2* Teacher's cushion p36, Adverts p38; *Book 3* Playground p38; *Book 4* Desk tidy p36, Election time p38. See also: *Book 4* Conservation area p22.

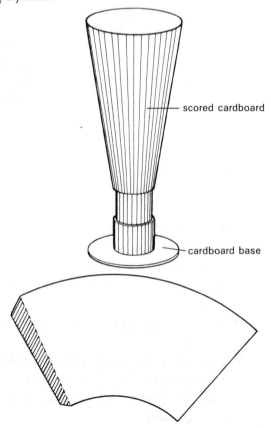

scored cardboard

cardboard base

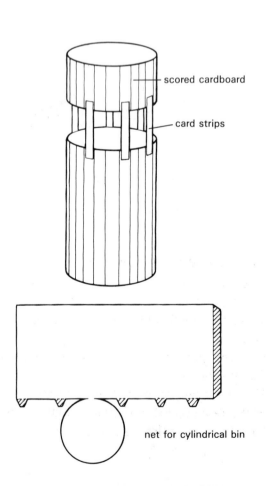

scored cardboard

card strips

net for cylindrical bin

Litter bin

Challenge

Can you design and make a litter bin for your school?

Design proposal

- Find out what sort of litter will need to be collected.
- What shape will your litter bin be?
- What size will it be?
- What shape and size will the opening of your bin be?
- Will it have a stand?
- Where will be the best place to put your litter bin?

Planning and making

- What materials will you need to make your model?
- How will you join the lid or stand to the bin?
- How will you make the opening for the litter?
- Will you decorate your bin?
- Draw your ideas carefully.
- Make sure that you use any tools carefully and safely.

Evaluating

- Have you designed and made a litter bin?
- Does your litter bin work?
- Do people use it?
- Is it attractive to look at?
- Is it easy to knock over (by children or animals)?
- Is the school a tidier place?

Further activities

- Can you design a device for picking up litter?
- Test where the best place is for a litter bin.
- Devise a litter-collecting rota to make sure that the school is tidy.
- Design a poster to encourage people not to drop litter.

Playground

Starting points

- Walk around the playground and discuss the good and bad points of current playground facilities.
- Collect data on other playground layouts, equipment and uses.
- Carefully measure the size, shape and area of the playground. Incorporate a survey into who uses what and times of use - present information in a chart or plan.

Materials ▲

Graphic materials, measuring equipment, junk materials, art straws, squared paper, card, video camera, video recorder, camera.

Teaching notes

- Discussion often reveals some dissatisfaction with the current playground. This can be developed into an analysis of what children do and what they want through a survey.

Photographs of the current playground can aid discussion. Video-recording playtimes from a height (eg from the school first floor) and replaying the tape at high speed graphically reveals what parts of the playground are heavily used and what they are used for. This may well bring to light gender differences in what children want from a playground, which can lead to fruitful discussion.

Key questions could include:
- What games are played? What games can't be played?
- Who uses the playground? Who needs to use it, but can't?
- When is it used? Is the time available for use fair?
- What surface is best (grass, tarmac or soft cushioning under equipment)?
- What equipment would improve the playground?
- Do we need seats, flower beds, trees or other elements.?

Design proposals can be carefully mapped on squared paper and prototype model playgrounds built using recycled materials on card. Attention will need to be paid to scale. Larger scale models of swings, slides, and seesaws can be built.

Invite design students from local colleges to do their own designs for the playground. Compare these with the children's ideas.

Extension activities

- Graphical work on most popular games.
- Measurement of length, width and area of games pitches.
- Study of pendulums (swings), levers (seesaws), and pushes-and-pulls, wheels and axles (roundabouts). Relate to work on forces (see Techniques pp51 and 55).
- Exploration of environmental issues in playground use (eg conservation area, recycling facilities).

Related investigations

SCHOOL theme: *Book 1* Musical instruments p36, School signs p38; *Book 2* Teacher's cushion p36, Adverts p38; *Book 3* Litter bin p36; *Book 4* Desk tidy p36, Election time p38. See also: *Book 4* Conservation area p22.

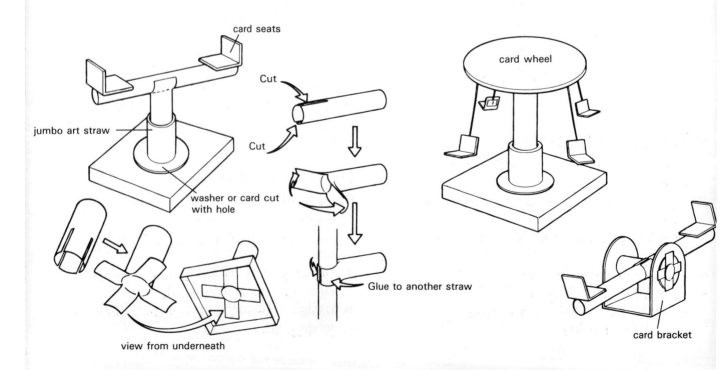

card seats

Cut

Cut

jumbo art straw

washer or card cut with hole

Glue to another straw

card wheel

card bracket

view from underneath

Playground

Challenge

Can you design a school playground in which all children can play safely and happily?

Design proposal

- Can you design a questionnaire to find out what children and adults think of the playground that you already have? You might include questions on:
  - what games children like to play
  - what equipment they use the most
  - what surface is best (grass, tarmac or something else)
  - what children can't do, but would like to do
  - whether girls or boys like the playground the most.
- How can you help make the playground safe?
- How will you space out your activities?
- Carefully draw a design of your playground.

Planning and making

- From your draft design, make a model of your playground.
- What materials will you need to make models of things to sit and play on?
- Will you mark out areas for team games? How will you do this?
- How will you make sure that children can share the play areas fairly?
- Will there be shelters for bad weather?

Evaluating

- Have you designed a school playground?
- Ask other people what they think of your model playground.
- Do girls and boys like your playground?
- Is there space for:
  - quiet activities?
  - noisy activities?
  - hiding?
  - climbing?
- Can you improve your playground equipment?
- Is your playground safe?

Further activities

- Can you design a nature area for your school playground?
- Can you design and make a booklet or poster about your playground?
- Can you design a plan for what to do during wet playtimes?
- Can you devise a set of rules to encourage good behaviour in the playground?

Kite

Starting points
- Collect examples or illustrations of kites to compare and contrast.
- Discuss where kite flying may take place locally and kites could be tested.
- Introduce research into flight by designing and making a spinner or parachute.

Materials ▲
Graphic materials, wooden dowelling, garden cane, hacksaws, polythene sheets (carrier bags or bin liners), string or thin gauge nylon, tissue paper, elastic bands, masking tape, thin card, plastic curtain rings, cotton fabric.

Teaching notes
The first kites were made in China and Japan. Different clans had different banners which were held aloft and left to stream in the wind. Kites were even used to lift criminals into the air to test the omens for long sea voyages or to spy on enemies. They have also been used in photography and weather forecasting.

A kite is controlled by a line which keeps the kite at an angle to the wind. The wind is deflected downward by the kite, providing a reaction force that equals the pull of the string. These equal but opposing forces keep the kite aloft.

Extension activities
- Design and make something else that will fly (eg a paper aeroplane, an aerofoil or a glider).
- Investigate the history of heavier-than-air flying machines.
- Design and make a hot air balloon.
- Design and make a machine operated by wind power (simple windmill).

Related investigations
TRANSPORT theme: *Book 1* Paper plane p40, Balloon rocket p42; *Book 2* Model boat p40, Spinner p42; *Book 3* Buggy p42; *Book 4* Level-crossing p40, Tipper truck p42. See also: *Book 3* Windmill p46.

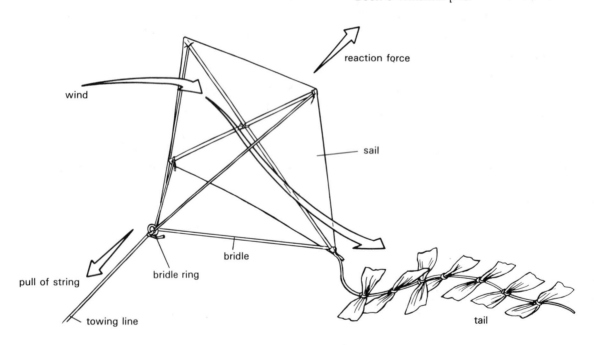

- See Techniques p54 for suggestions for kite making.

Key questions could include:
- What makes a kite rise?
- What is it that keeps a kite in the air?
- Do kites need a tail to help them fly?
- What is the best shape for a kite?

Kite

Challenge

Can you design and make a kite that will fly outdoors?

Design proposal

- What shape will your kite be?
- Will your kite need a tail?
- Will your kite need a frame?
- Carefully draw your design based upon the simplest shape.

Planning and making

- What materials will you use? Consider:
  - string
  - polythene
  - wooden dowelling
  - garden canes.
- How will you attach the bridle (a set of strings that keeps the towing line pulling from the centre of the kite) to the kite?
- How will you attach your towing line to the bridle?

Evaluating

- Have you designed and made a kite?
- Test your kite. Does it fly well?
- How can you improve it? Can you:
  - make it lighter?
  - change its size?
  - change its shape?
  - make it stronger?
  - change the tail?
  - attach the towing line in a different place?

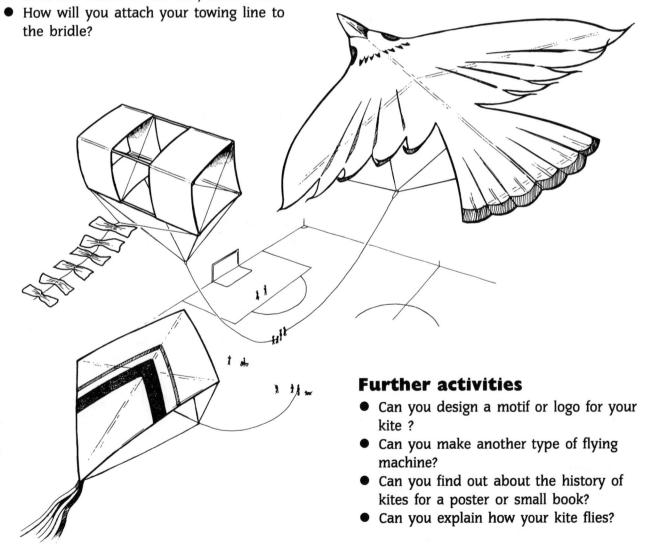

Further activities

- Can you design a motif or logo for your kite ?
- Can you make another type of flying machine?
- Can you find out about the history of kites for a poster or small book?
- Can you explain how your kite flies?

▲ WARNING: Never fly your kite near overhead wires!

Buggy

Starting points

- Evaluate a collection of toys brought by the children involving movement.
- Close observational drawings of toys with moving parts, concentrating on connections (eg how axles are fixed to chassis).
- Display and discuss illustrations of various types of moving vehicles.

Materials ▲

Graphic materials, junk materials, dowelling, hacksaws, bench hooks, wood, cotton reels, elastic bands, lolly sticks, clothes pegs, hole punch, card wheels, artstraws, straws, construction kits, plastic tubing, old Biros, rubber washers, cardboard, craft knives, cutting mats, metal rules.

Teaching notes

Discuss what kind of power can move a toy vehicle. Challenge children to design a vehicle that can move a fixed distance (eg 1 m) or one that stops when it meets an obstacle.

Key questions could include:
- What do objects need in order to move? (A force: push, pull or twist.)
- What source of energy can be used to move the vehicle? (Wind, balloon, battery.)
- What stops the vehicle from moving? (Friction or an obstacle.)
- How can we make movement as easy as possible? (Use of bearings.)
- How can we make the chassis (main frame of the car), wheels, axles (the shafts upon which the wheels turn) and bearings (the hole in which the axle rotates)?
- For starting points for buggies see Techniques pp51, 60 and 62.

Basic Principles
- Things need energy in order to move. Energy can be thought of as stored work. To apply energy we need to work (eg twisting or pulling an elastic band). This is stored until the energy is released, causing the buggy to move.
- Friction is a force which prevents surfaces sliding over each other. It opposes movement. It is caused by tiny irregularities on the surfaces of everything. Magnifying the smoothest of surfaces would reveal:

rolling friction

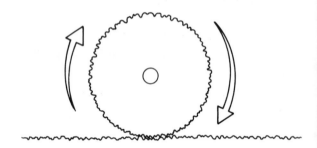

In the second example showing a wheel, one can see how rounded surfaces reduce friction. There are fewer irregularities in contact with each other, and as the rounded surface rolls it crushes the irregularities on the flat surface, thereby reducing friction. Friction can, of course, be very beneficial. Without it we could be unable to move.

Extension activities
- Study the history of movement on land.
- The consequences of a world without friction, where all surfaces slide over each other.

Related investigations

TRANSPORT theme: *Book 1* Paper plane p40, Balloon rocket p42; *Book 2* Model boat p40, Spinner p42; *Book 3* Kite p40; *Book 4* Level-crossing p40, Tipper truck p42. See also: *Book 1* Bridges p8; *Book 3* Cranes p44.

3-wheeled buggy

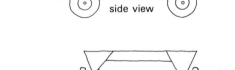

side view

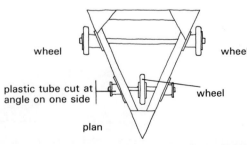

wheel   wheel

plastic tube cut at
angle on one side   wheel

plan

sliding friction

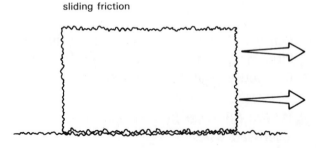

Buggy

Challenge

Can you design and make a buggy that will move at least one metre using energy from elastic bands?

Design proposal

- How will you design and make the chassis?
- How will you design and make the axle?
- How will you attach the wheels?
- How will you make sure that the wheels spin freely?
- How will you attach the elastic bands to drive the wheels?
- Draw a detailed sketch to show how you will solve these problems.

Evaluating

- Have you made a buggy that can move one metre?
- Record how far your buggy can move. Repeat with different trials.
- On what surface does your buggy work best? Test out your buggy on different surfaces and record your results.
- Can you improve your buggy in any way?

Planning and making

- What materials will you use for:
  - the chassis?
  - the axle?
  - the wheels?
- How will you make sure that the materials don't rub too much against each other and stop the buggy moving?

Further activities

- Can you make your buggy move one metre and then stop?
- Can you make your buggy move using a different source of energy?
- Can you design and make a buggy that you can steer?
- Can you design and make a body shape for your buggy?
- Name your buggy and design an advert for it, showing other people how it works.

Cranes

Starting points
- Investigate how the Pyramids or Stonehenge were built (without cranes).
- Collect and study model cranes or pictures of cranes.
- Visit a building site (remember safety factors) or hire firm for close observational drawings of cranes.

Materials ▲
Graphic materials, junk materials, wood, card, masking tape, weights, artstraws, string, fishing line, balloons, clay, Plasticine, syringes, 3 mm plastic tubing, magnets, hacksaws, bench hooks.

Teaching notes

The crane was invented by the Romans. Previously, earth ramps were used to manouevre large objects such as obelisks (Egyptians) or stones (Stonehenge).

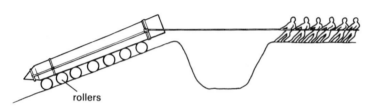

rollers

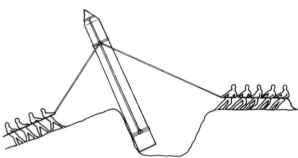

Introduce the work by discussing the problems faced by these builders.

Investigate counterweights. Possibly the earliest counter-balanced crane was the ancient Egyptian *Shadoof,* still in use today to irrigate land on either side of the Nile. A simple see-saw type version of this can be made from art straws with a pin or straightened paper clip used as a fulcrum. This is an example of a first-class lever (see Techniques p55).

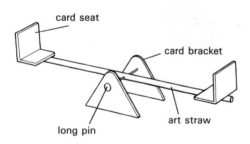

card seat

card bracket

long pin

art straw

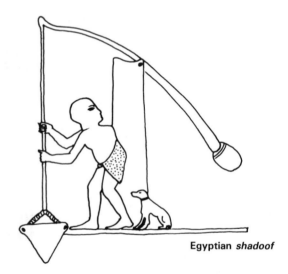

Egyptian *shadoof*

Alternatively, a pneumatic mechanism (using the power of air) or hydraulic mechanism (using the power of water) can be attempted (see Techniques pp56 and 57 and *Book 4* Tipper truck p42). The work can be developed by a study of pulleys (see Techniques p60).

Key questions could include:
- What things do we use that make lifting easier? (See-saws to demonstrate leverage, counterbalancing.)
- What can we use to pick up weights? (Hook, magnet or basket.)
- How do real-life cranes work? (Toy cranes, building-site, video material.)

Extension activities
- Construct a model earth ramp to show how large objects can be moved.
- Investigate history of moving heavy objects.
- Design and make a lift using a pulley system.
- Design and make a mobile crane (mounted on chassis, see *Book 3* Buggy p42).

Related investigations
WORLD OF WORK theme: *Book 1* Carrier bag p44, School stall p46; *Book 2* Milk or paper round p44, Coin sorter p46; *Book 3* Windmill p46; *Book 4* Conveyor belt p44, Water mill p46. See also: *Book 3* Buggy p42; *Book 4* Tipper truck p42.

- See R. Fisher (ed) *Problem Solving in Primary Schools* (Simon & Schuster Education) p137ff · How did they move the stones?

Cranes

Challenge

Can you design and make a crane that will lift a load of 200 g 25 cm into the air?

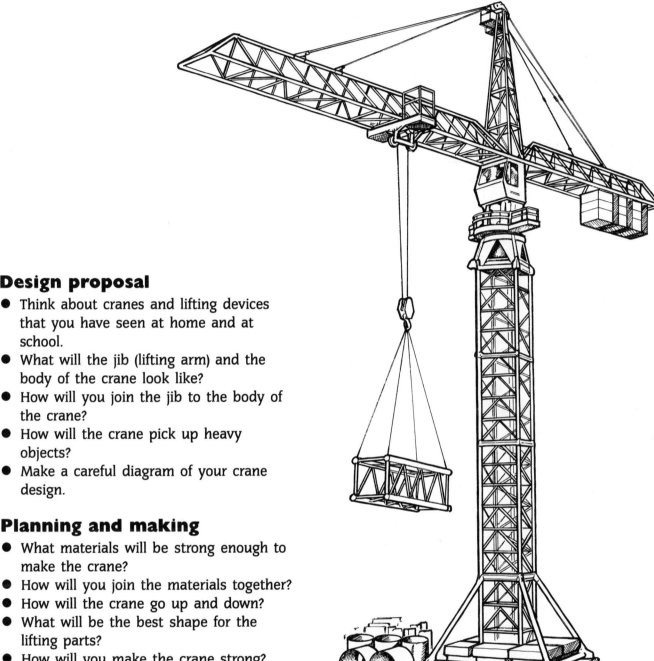

Design proposal

- Think about cranes and lifting devices that you have seen at home and at school.
- What will the jib (lifting arm) and the body of the crane look like?
- How will you join the jib to the body of the crane?
- How will the crane pick up heavy objects?
- Make a careful diagram of your crane design.

Planning and making

- What materials will be strong enough to make the crane?
- How will you join the materials together?
- How will the crane go up and down?
- What will be the best shape for the lifting parts?
- How will you make the crane strong?

Evaluating

- Have you designed and made a crane?
- Test out how much weight your crane will carry.
- Does your crane work?
- Could you improve it by strengthening any part of it?
- Would it work better using different materials?
- What uses can you think of for your crane?

Further activities

- Design and make something to make your crane move.
- Design and make another lifting machine, for example:
  - a lift
  - a fork lift truck
  - an escalator.
- Design and make something to lift water from a well.

Windmill

Starting points
- Observe the effects of wind on natural objects such as trees or manufactured objects such as weather vanes.
- Display and evaluate machines with rotating parts.
- Collect pictures and books of old and new windmills.

Materials ▲
Graphic materials, card, beads, pins, wood, hacksaws, bench hooks, string, fishing line, First Gear Plus (construction kit), junk materials, cardboard, card wheels, lollipop sticks.

Teaching notes
Wind is air moving over the Earth. Demonstrate the energy of wind by making a toy windmill.

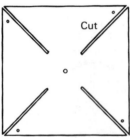

Cut

thin square card

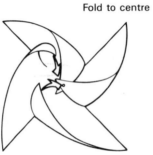

Fold to centre

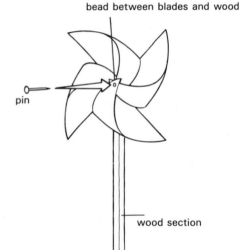

bead between blades and wood

pin

wood section

Ask the children to blow on one windmill sail to see what happens. If they walk across and create a draught, they will find that the sails rotate much faster because moving air is acting on all the sails, rather than just one. This is the reason why windmills have many sails.

Key questions could include:
- If we blow at the windmill, why do the sails rotate?
- Why do the sails rotate in only one direction?
- Can a windmill be designed and made that will rotate in another direction?

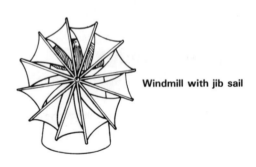

Windmill with jib sail

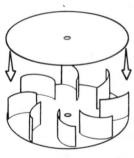
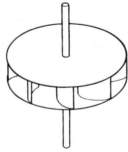

Wind turbine

Develop the toy windmill by challenging children to make it do some work, eg lifting up a small object.
- Make a wind turbine using card. Curved blades work best (increased area for moving air to act on).
- Develop the work to include the use of gear wheels to change the direction of movement (First Gear Plus is particularly effective). See Techniques p60.

Extension activities
- Study of different kinds of windmills, eg in the Mediterranean; windmill sails tend to be made out of cloth (jib sails) like the sails of boats.
- Design and make sails using fabrics which can be dyed or printed.
- Tell the story of Don Quixote tilting at windmills.

Related investigations
WORLD OF WORK theme: *Book 1* Carrier bag p44, School stall p46; *Book 2* Milk or paper round p44, Coin sorter p46; *Book 3* Cranes p44; *Book 4* Conveyor belt p44, Water mill p46. See also: *Book 2* Weather Station p22.

Windmill

Challenge

Can you design and make a windmill that will do some kind of work?

Design proposal

- List or chart the ways in which the wind can be used to help us to do work.
- Sketch your design for making something that will rotate in the wind.
- Can you use the turning movement to pick up something?

Planning and making

- What materials will you use? Remember that they should be:
  - strong
  - flexible
  - easy to work with.
- What part of the windmill will be turned by the wind?
- How will you keep your windmill fixed to the ground?

Evaluating

- Have you made a windmill that works?
- Test your windmill to see where it works best.
- Can you improve your windmill? Think about changing:
  - the shape of the sails
  - the material of the sails
  - the number of sails.
- Can you make the sails spin more freely?

Further activities

- Design and make a boat with sails. What is the best shape for a sail?
- Find out as much as you can about windmills. Can you use what you have found out to make a better windmill?
- Design and make a device to measure:
  - wind speed
  - wind direction.
- Can you find out about the Beaufort Scale?

Techniques

MAKING BOOKS

Tools and materials

Paper (various grades and colours), newspaper, card (recycled greyboard is ideal), cold water paste, thick brush, needles, thread, paper trimmer, bookbinding tape.

Prepare all surfaces by covering them with newspaper or clean waste paper. The children should wear overalls (old shirts).

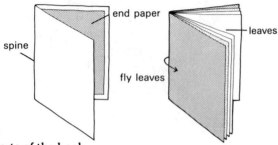

Parts of the book

Hard-backed book (A5)

To make the inside leaves, collate four sheets (or more) of A4 paper and two sheets of coloured or previously marbled paper and trim 5 mm off the top and side. Enclose the A4 paper with the coloured paper and fold in half. Sew the sheets together with the knot on the outside of the leaves.

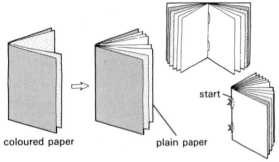

Prepare the cover paper of the book using marbling, printing or stencilling (see pp53, 58 and 59). Cut the cover paper in half, ensuring that each piece is at least 2 cm larger than A5 all the way round. Lay the cover paper face down on a pile of single sheets of clean waste paper. Paste liberally, brushing outward from the centre. Place the A5 cover board (recycled grey board) on the middle of the cover paper, pressing firmly. Cut a 45 degree mitre on all corners, allowing approximately 3 mm between the mitre and board. Fold the flaps to the inside of the cover.

Repeat for back cover of book.

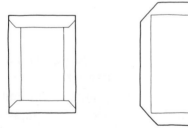

Place the bookbinding tape, sticky side up, on clean waste paper and carefully lay the covered board on this sheet, leaving a gap slightly larger than the width of the prepared inside leaves. Fold over the bookbinding tape top and bottom.

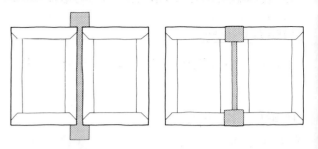

Open out the prepared inside leaves and paste the outside of the end papers. Align the right-hand edge of the end paper with the middle of the bookbinding tape and firmly smooth down to affix to cover. Cover with clean waste paper. Repeat with the other end paper. Close the book and leave to dry.

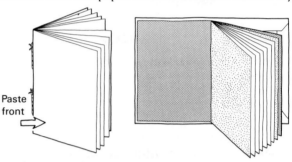

Book cover with spine (A4)

Cut the spine of the book from board slightly thicker than the inside leaves of the book and the same height as the cut coverboards. Lay the coverboards and spine on previously decorated cover paper. Leave a gap of 4 mm between the spine and the covers, and 2 cm from the coverboard to the outside of the cover papers.

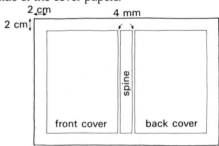

Cut a 45 degree mitre on all corners, leaving a 3 mm gap from the corner of the coverboards. Fold and paste.

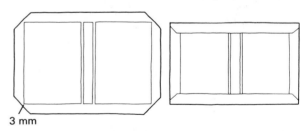

Reinforce the spine with a spare piece of paper the same height as the book pages.

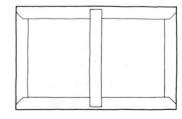

Concertina book

The book cover with a spine can be used to make a concertina book. Fold a long strip of paper in a concertina fashion and carefully paste in the front of the book, aligning the right side of the front page with the right side of the coverboard. Repeat for the back page.

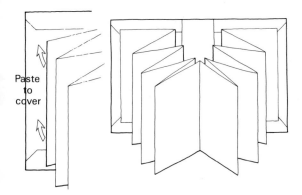

Pop-up books

Use the book cover with a spine for pop-up books. It is best to make pop-up books by treating each page separately, as if making a series of pop-up cards (see Pop-up and moving cards p49), and then carefully gluing the edges together to make a book, keeping the glue clear of any mechanism. Fix fly and end papers to the book and glue the whole collection into the book cover with a spine, having carefully matched the width of the spine to the thickness of the contents.

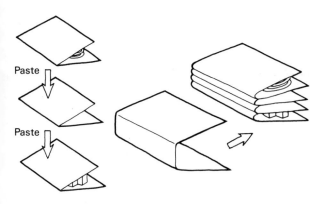

Decorated covers – paper

Decorate the covers, fly leaves and end papers using marbling, printing and stencilling techniques (see pp53 and 59). It is generally advisable to decorate the covers before making the books, but decorated covers can be stuck on finished books. Leaving a 25 mm gap between the decorated paper and the edge gives a pleasing effect. Ensure that the pasted paper dries under pressure. Wax rubbings of textured surfaces, such as tree barks and walls, painted over with a very diluted solution of Indian ink, make simple effective covers. Waterproof the covers by applying in small circular movements any kind of wax polish with a pad of clean cloth. After a few minutes drying, polish the paper with another clean cloth. Repeat as often as desired to achieve a smooth, high-gloss cover. Alternatively, use a spray polish and buff with a clean cloth.

Decorated covers – fabric

Printed and tie-dyed natural fabrics make attractive and interesting book covers (see Printing on fabric p57). Use a fabric glue, such as Copydex, as an adhesive.

POP-UP AND MOVING CARDS

Tools and materials

Scissors, thick card, thin card, ruler, spirit-based glue (eg UHU or Bostick All Purpose – paste or pva will distort the card) or Pritt Stick, paper clips, paper fasteners, single-hole punch. Optional: circle or compass cutter, craft knife, cutting mat, eyeletting tool, eyelets.

Techniques

To make a scoring guide for folding card:

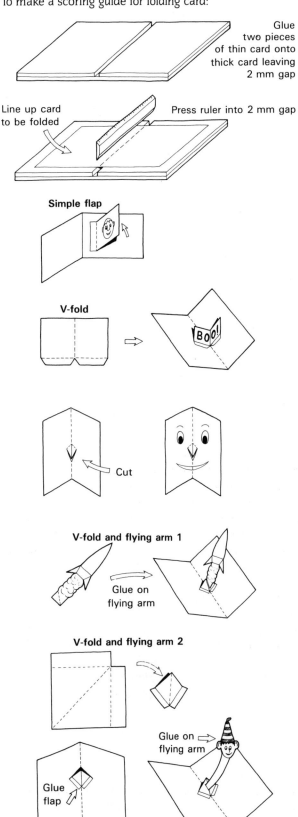

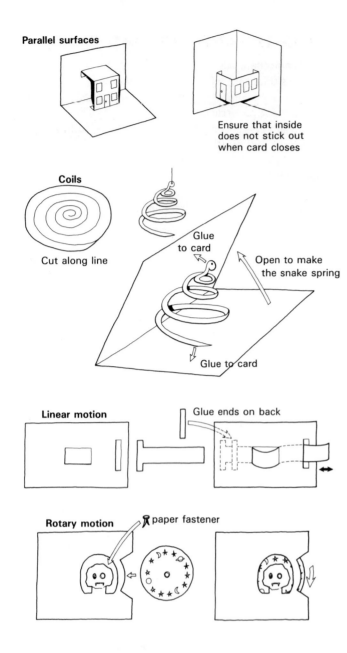

Parallel surfaces

Ensure that inside does not stick out when card closes

Coils

Cut along line

Glue to card

Open to make the snake spring

Glue to card

Linear motion

Glue ends on back

Rotary motion   paper fastener

CARDBOARD

Tools and materials

Craft knives, large scissors, rotary cutters, safety snips, cutting mats (A3 size or larger), metal rules (ridged for safety), hole punch, eyelet punch, eyelets, pva adhesive, paper fasteners (butterfly type). Optional: wheel punch, hammer, compass cutter, glue gun, hand drill.

After newspaper, corrugated cardboard is the cheapest and most widely available material. Arrange with local shops or offices for you to collect on a regular basis. Look for clean, smooth surfaces – crushed cardboard is relatively useless. Try to get the same kind of cardboard each time. The most suitable comes from boxes holding A4 paper. This is a single-wall type which is strong, flexible and relatively easy to cut.

single wall

Cutting the cardboard into standardised A4 or A5 shapes will give you a 'currency' of cardboard to work with if you want the children to cost materials in the designing and making process. The cut cardboard can be easily stored in cardboard boxes, ready for use in the classroom.

Techniques

The basic cutting tool is the craft knife or rotary cutter, but strong scissors or safety snips can be used with younger children. Always use a non-slip cutting mat to protect surfaces, together with a metal safety rule. This has central ridge to hold it in place well clear of the cutting blade. Train the children carefully, ensuring that fingers are never placed in the path of the cutting blade. Keep the cutting angle close to the board for a smooth, clean cut:

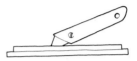

It is worth experimenting with a few techniques yourself before training the children in their use. Cut strips in varying lengths and widths. Glue strips together for extra strength and thickness.

Numbering the fluted lines will enable the children to score the cardboard accurately (cut through one layer of the cardboard) to make solid shapes. Challenge the children to make pillars with different numbers of sides. The sides can be joined inside with masking tape or by gluing an extra flap. Test the pillars for strength. Use scored and folded cardboard as a hinge:

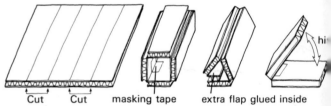

Cut   Cut   masking tape   extra flap glued inside

To make the cardboard flexible (eg for making cog wheels and driving belts), soak one layer of the cardboard with a damp cloth or sponge until the plain layer can be peeled away. The success of this depends upon the amount of glue used in the manufacture of the cardboard. It is best to do this after the cardboard has been cut to size:

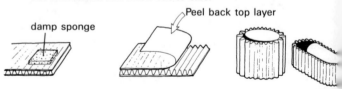

Peel back top layer

damp sponge

Make cylindrical forms by scoring parallel to the fluting:

Score the cardboard to make nets of various solid shapes. For ideas, open out a variety of manufactured boxes. These can be reassembled inside out for modelling purposes.

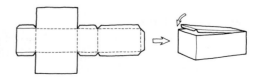

Punch holes into the cardboard using a hole punch or card drill. Reinforce the holes using an eyelet punch and eyelets. Join strips of card using paper fasteners:

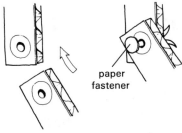

paper fastener

Join cardboard strips end to end by pushing matchsticks or thin dowelling into the fluted edges:

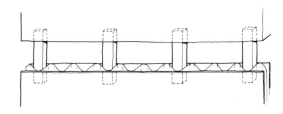

Corriflute or Correx is basically plastic cardboard. Use the same techniques. The materials have the advantage of being waterproof and brightly coloured. The disadvantage is that they cost money.

Make a simple buggy with a sheet of cardboard with clothes pegs as bearings glued on. Thread dowelling through pen casings for an axle.

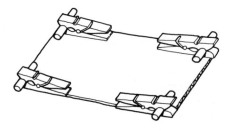

Make wheels using a wheel punch or compass cutter. Drill a hole in a small piece of wood or cardboard and glue to the centre of the wheel. Fix to the dowelling:

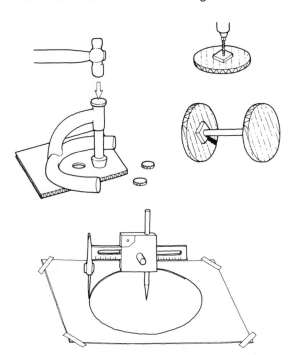

WHEELS AND AXLES

Use tin cans, tin lids, film cannisters, sponge balls as well as the following:

Cotton reels

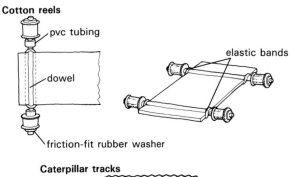

pvc tubing

elastic bands

dowel

friction-fit rubber washer

Caterpillar tracks

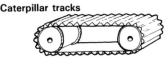

Margarine tubs and cheese box lids

garden cane

Blu-tack

Strengthening cardboard

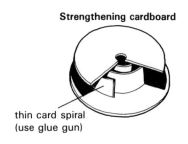

thin card spiral
(use glue gun)

Drinks bottle tops

Airflow balls

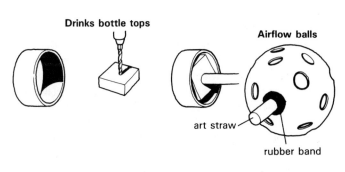

art straw

rubber band

Double wheel for flanges

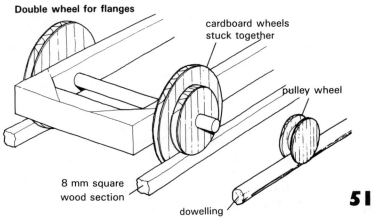

cardboard wheels
stuck together

pulley wheel

8 mm square
wood section

dowelling

51

CLAY

Tools and materials
Clay, large board, clay modelling tools, rolling pin, flat wooden slats, plastic beaker, paint brush, water.

Kneading
Kneading prepares the clay for use by expelling air and making it pliable. Place a brick-sized piece of clay on a wooden board and make it into an oval shape. Press the heels of the hands on both sides of the clay with a downward movement away from the body.

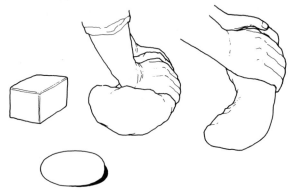

Pull the clay up towards the body with the fingers and repeat the pressing movement, keeping the process as rhythmic as possible using the force of the whole body. Repeat about 25 times until the clay becomes plastic and easy to work. The finished clay should look like a bull's head (this method is called Bull's Head Kneading).

Coil pots
Roll out the clay on a wooden board. Press an upturned plastic beaker into the clay to cut a circular base. Score grooves around this base using a pointed tool. Brush slip (a mixture of clay and a little water) over the grooves. Roll out a piece of clay to make a coil of even thickness. Press the coil firmly on to the base over the grooves. Smooth down the coil with a wooden tool so that it fuses with the base inside the coil. Build up the pot in a spiral, fusing each coil to the one below it:

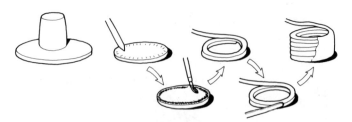

The shape of the pot can be altered by pressing from the inside with the handle of a clay tool, holding the hand on the outside to protect the pot. Make the pot smooth by rolling very thin coils and attaching them between the seams of the larger coils as the pot is built up. Smooth with hand and a wooden hand tool:

Slab method
Flatten out a piece of clay using a rolling pin resting on two wooden slats. Using a piece of wood as a guide, cut the clay into five sections to make the base and walls of a box. (The flat sections may alternatively be used as tiles.) Brush slip around the edges of the base of the box. Roll out a thin coil of clay and smooth it between the wall and the base. Fuse the coil, wall and base with a wooden clay tool:

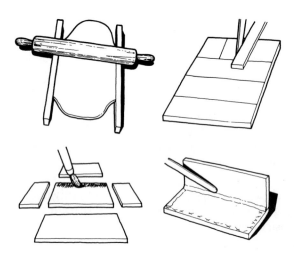

Repeat for the other walls, fusing coils in the seams between the walls and the base. Smooth over the joints on the outside of the box with a wooden clay tool. Straighten the sides of the box by smoothing them against a piece of wood and level off the top edges. Cut the slab to size for the lid. Attach two long thin slabs to form the flanges, leaving 1.5 mm clearance all around:

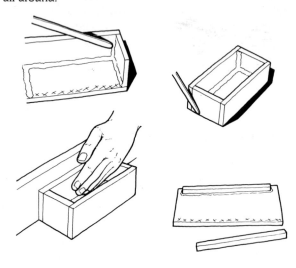

Turn the lid over and attach the handles:

The coil pot and slab box are now ready for decorating with clay tools, glazing and firing.

FABRIC CRAYONS

Fabric crayons are available from educational suppliers. They are inexpensive, very simple to use and last a long time, giving very pleasing results.

Tools and materials
Fabric crayons, white paper, electric iron, newspaper.

Techniques
Draw your design on white paper, bearing in mind that the design will be transferred in reverse. Press hard when crayoning, blowing away any crayon specks.

Make an ironing pad by placing a sheet of white paper over several layers of newspaper. Alternatively, use an ironing board.

The best results are obtained by using synthetic fabrics, but the process works well on natural fabrics. When transferring a design to a garment rather than a single layer of fabric, protect the back by placing several sheets of white paper between the inside front and back of the garment.

Lay the design face down on the fabric. Place another sheet of white paper over the back of the design. Using the 'cotton' setting on the electric iron, press steadily over the entire design. Do not move the iron back and forth or the design will be blurred. Keep pressing the iron down until the image is slightly visible through the back of the white paper. Remove the design paper carefully to reveal the finished transfer.

PASTEL FABRIC CRAYONS

Sometimes called pastel dye sticks, these work best on natural fabrics. Avoid using 100% synthetics as they do not stand up to the high ironing temperatures. For best results, wash and iron the fabric or garment and pin it to a piece of cardboard. Apply the pastel to the fabric in one direction only to ensure a smooth, unbroken line of colour. Colours can be blended together using a finger tip. Cover the design with a sheet of clean white paper and press over with a hot iron on the 'cotton' setting.

With both processes the fabric can be machine-washed using warm water and a gentle action.

This type of work is particularly suitable for designing curtains or furniture covers for a model house, book covers, motifs of all kinds. Let the children use their imaginations!

MARBLING

Tools and materials
Marbling inks, large shallow tray, water, paper, white spirit, pencils, detergent.

Techniques
The appeal of marbling lies in its simplicity and unpredictability of the finished result. Every print is different.

The simplest method of marbling uses oil-based marbling inks, which are available from educational suppliers. These are extremely economical to use and give impressive results. They will not wash out of children's clothing. Ensure that protective clothing is used and contact is avoided with eyes and mouth. Cover any surfaces used with newspaper.

Cover the base of the tray with water to a depth of approximately 2 cm.

Drop two or three drops of the chosen ink on to the surface of the water and allow them to spread. Experiment with two or three colours. The most pleasing effects tend to be with no more than three or four colours.

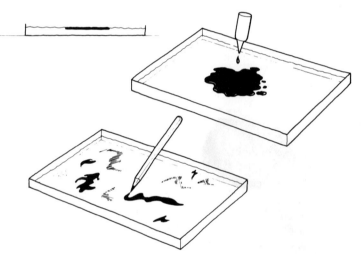

Gently swirl the colours together with the end of a pencil. When the ripples have settled, gently lay a sheet of paper (smaller than the size of the tray) on the surface of the water. Peel off when the edges of the paper are beginning to curl up. Place the paper, marbled side up, on a flat surface to dry.

More than one print can be taken from each application of ink, but successive prints will be paler. Experiment with different grades and colours of paper.

Residual traces of ink on the surface of the water can be mopped up by drawing a sheet of newspaper across the top of the water.

Clean any equipment used with white spirit followed by detergent with water.

The finished prints make excellent covers and end papers for books, interesting gift wraps, wallpapers for model houses – the list is endless!

It is possible to use plain fabrics in the process. Treat the washed and ironed fabric as paper. The results tend to be extremely pale, however.

FLIGHT

Paper aircraft 1

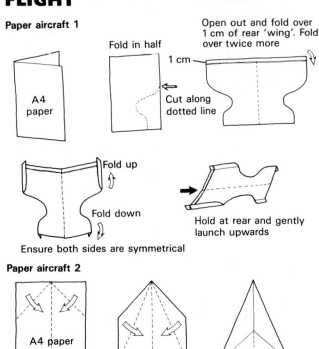

Fold in half

Open out and fold over 1 cm of rear 'wing'. Fold over twice more

1 cm

A4 paper

Cut along dotted line

Fold up

Fold down

Ensure both sides are symmetrical

Hold at rear and gently launch upwards

Paper aircraft 2

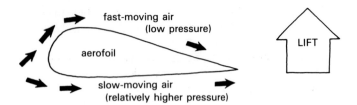

A4 paper

Cut flaps

Fold along dotted lines

Try to see how performance changes with flaps up or down

Kites

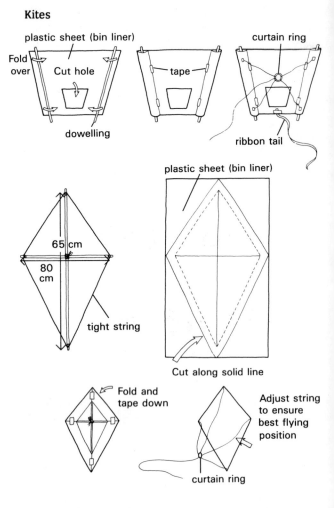

plastic sheet (bin liner)

Fold over

Cut hole

tape

curtain ring

dowelling

ribbon tail

plastic sheet (bin liner)

65 cm

80 cm

tight string

Cut along solid line

Fold and tape down

Adjust string to ensure best flying position

curtain ring

Principles of flight

A Swiss scientist, Daniel Bernouilli, discovered that fast moving air creates a lower pressure than slower moving air. Aeroplanes have specially shaped wings called aerofoils. The upper curved surface is longer than the lower, often flat, surface. Air has to travel faster over the upper surface, creating a lower pressure on the top of the aerofoil than under it. This produces *lift* which pushes the aerofoil upwards.

fast-moving air (low pressure)

aerofoil

LIFT

slow-moving air (relatively higher pressure)

Jet propulsion

Newton's third law of motion states that for every action there is an equal and opposite reaction. Air rushing out of the balloon opening causes an equal and opposite reaction. The balloon shoots forward. This is called *thrust*.

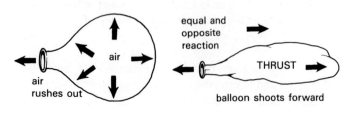

equal and opposite reaction

air

air rushes out

THRUST

balloon shoots forward

How a spinner works

The spinner is a type of autogyro. Air resistance forces the arms of the spinner up. The shape of the spinner means that equal and opposing forces are acting at different points about the same pivot or axis. This makes the spinner spin. The principle can best be demonstrated by using a pair of chopsticks to pick up a cork. If the chopsticks are not placed directly opposite each other, the cork will spin in much the same manner as the autogyro.

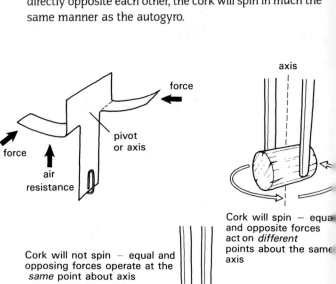

force

pivot or axis

force

air resistance

axis

Cork will spin — equal and opposite forces act on *different* points about the same axis

Cork will not spin — equal and opposing forces operate at the *same* point about axis

LEVERS

A lever is a rigid bar or beam which can turn about a fixed point (pivot or fulcrum). Levers can change the direction in which a force acts. They make work easier. Less effort can produce the same results by increasing the distance from the fulcrum. However, the effort has to move a greater distance to shift the load. You gain in force what you pay in distance. There are three types of lever:

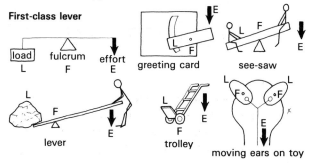

First-class lever

greeting card   see-saw

lever   trolley   moving ears on toy

The effort and load are on opposite sides of the fulcrum with the forces acting in opposite directions.

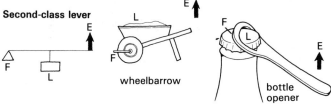

Second-class lever

wheelbarrow   bottle opener

The effort and the load are on the same side of the fulcrum with the load between the effort and the fulcrum moving in the same direction as the effort.

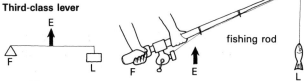

Third-class lever

fishing rod

The effort and load are on the same side of the fulcrum with the effort between the load and the fulcrum moving in the same direction as the load.

Levers can be investigated through work with pop-up and moving cards, seesaws, cranes, moving toys, mobiles, balances, tipper trucks and buggies.

MUSICAL INSTRUMENTS

A starting point for making musical instruments is the evaluation of manufactured instruments, focusing on how they work. Children can then design and make their own instruments using a variety of material. Here are some suggested starting points:

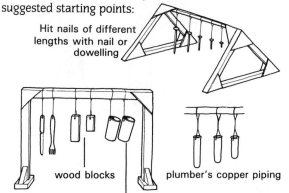

Hit nails of different lengths with nail or dowelling

wood blocks   plumber's copper piping

tin cans (empty or filled with dried peas)

Beaters, shakers and rattlers

Drill holes

Fasten with string

drinks bottle

Drill holes

yoghurt pots

cloth, plastic bag or paper

Try dried peas, rice, gravel or pebbles

elastic band

margarine tubs

Shake a large piece of cardboard (wobble board)

Pluckers   elastic bands

screw eyes   wood block

Stagger hole positions to vary 'string' length

Make holes with bradawl

thick dowel (experiment with different positions)

Use cut elastic bands

elastic bands   wood beading

wooden box (try different sizes)

matchbox

Tie 'string' to matchstick

screw eyes   elastic   Swing length of thick plastic tubing

wood

Blow across

water   milk bottles

Strike carefully with nail or dowelling

Try different container shapes (china or glass)

NEEDLEWORK

Tools and materials

Fabric, dressmaking thread, embroidery thread, sharp needles (for most work), crewel needles (for embroidery), thimble, scissors.

Basic stitches

Tacking

This is a temporary stitch used to hold edges together. Before starting, pin the materials in position. Make the gap between stitches about 1 cm.

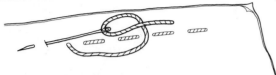

Running stitch (gathering)

This is a small stitch, used for seams or edges. Use a long needle and thread long enough to make gathering the material possible. When gathering the material with two rows of stitches, complete the two rows of stitching before pulling the threads together.

Back stitch

Stronger than the running stitch, this can be used for seams. Work from right to left, on top of the cloth, and left to right under it, first bringing the needle up, then back down the previous hole and up again a stitch in front of the first hole, with about 3 mm-stitch lengths.

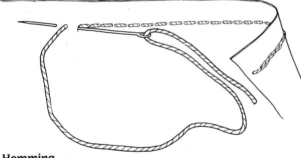

Hemming

This is a useful stitch which should hardly show on the finished material. On the back of the material, the stitches should be slanting. On the front, they should be small and regular.

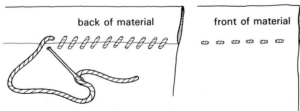

back of material   front of material

Oversewing

This is used for joining folded edges together. Work from right to left, keeping the stitches small and close together.

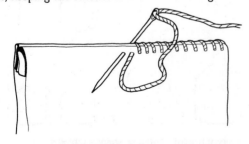

Blanket stitch

Use this for joining thick materials. Work from left to right, keeping the edge towards you with even spaces between each stitch. Fasten on with tiny stitches, taking the needle through near the edge then about 6 mm above to the right.

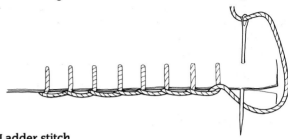

Ladder stitch

This is useful for sewing up soft toys and joining up two folded edges. Make the stitches inside the fold, pulling tightly to close the gap. Fasten under one edge, bringing the needle out to make a small stitch on the other fold.

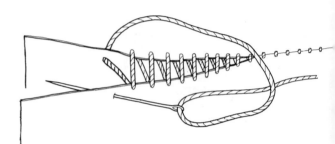

PNEUMATICS

In a pneumatic system, air is used to transmit force (pressure) from one place to another. Such systems are used for remote control.

Syringes can be used to provide control. They are available in a range of sizes. Large ones can push out small ones with great force. Ensure care is taken in their use. Attach one syringe fully compressed to the other slightly compressed, using 3 mm pvc tubing. Use elastic bands or masking tape to secure the syringes. Syringes can be hidden inside devices.

▲ Warning: Children should never pick up syringes outside of school.

Investigate to see if syringes can pull as well as push.

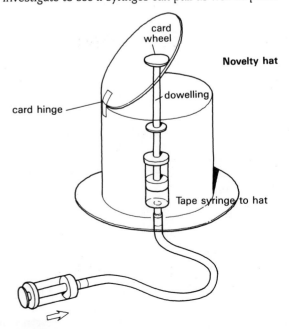

card wheel

Novelty hat

card hinge   dowelling

Tape syringe to hat

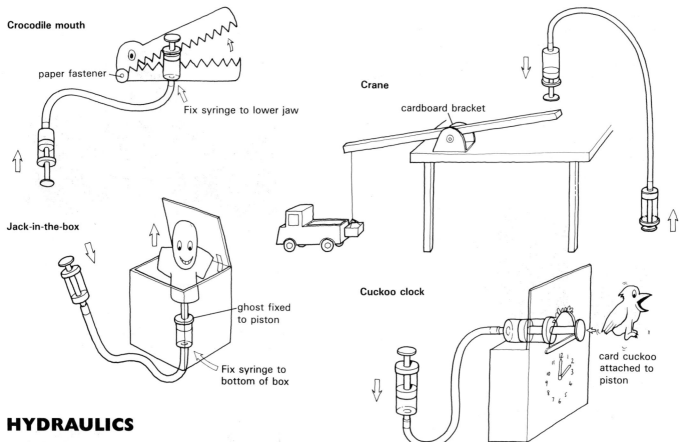

Crocodile mouth

paper fastener

Fix syringe to lower jaw

Jack-in-the-box

ghost fixed to piston

Fix syringe to bottom of box

Crane

cardboard bracket

Cuckoo clock

card cuckoo attached to piston

HYDRAULICS

In a hydraulic system, water or oil is used to transmit force (pressure) from one place to another, as in a car's brakes. Because liquids are virtually incompressible, they can sustain large forces (high pressures).

Fill the syringes underwater to prevent air getting inside. Attach one fully compressed syringe to the tubing and pull out the plunger to fill the syringe with water. Fully compress the other syringe and attach to the tubing.

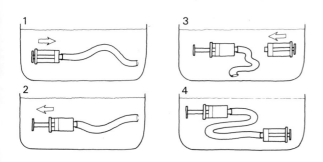

Switch

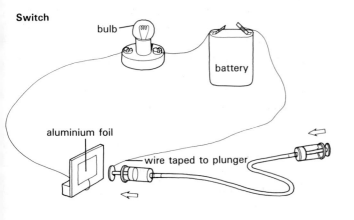

bulb

battery

aluminium foil

wire taped to plunger

PRINTING ON FABRIC

Textile printing was used in Egypt, India and Java over 2500 years ago. The techniques explained here are surprisingly easy to master yet give effective and satisfying results.

Tools and materials

Fabrics, newspaper, newsprint, old blanket, paint brushes (various sizes to 25 mm), detergent, pins, printing rollers, printing trays (or glass sheet).

Techniques

The most effective fabric to use is pure cotton, which can be collected by the children (old sheets or pillow cases) or purchased very cheaply from department stores, markets or educational suppliers. Also consider linen, calico or cambric. Ensure that the fabric has been thoroughly washed and ironed flat before use. Whenever possible, pin the fabric down before printing.

Fabric inks can be purchased from educational suppliers (eg Polyprint from NES Arnold).

Cover the working surface with an old blanket. Place newspaper on top of this. It is useful to have a pile of sheets of newspaper cut to approximately A4 size to place immediately over any spillages or excess ink. To conserve fabric, use newsprint for experimentation with techniques and variations of pattern. Once the children are satisfied with the results, printing on fabric can begin.

Effective patterns can be made by overprinting the fabric with different colours. Always finish the design in one colour before progressing to the next. This simplifies the process and maintains a rhythm about the printing. Use the lightest inks first, as these will be easy to print over.

Scrap objects

Additional materials: scrap objects, masking tape, doilies, rolling pin, fabric adhesive, wood offcuts, pva adhesive.

Use any objects with an interesting surface (corks, dice, washers, cogs, bottle tops, leaves, glass or plastic jars). Press the raised surface of an object into the ink, or apply the ink with a paint brush. Press on to the fabric. Make a more permanent block by sticking the object to a wooden block using fabric adhesive or wood glue.

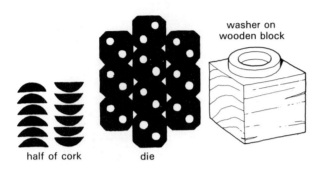

half of cork   die   washer on wooden block

Masking tape

Place the tape directly on the fabric in the pattern desired and ink up the fabric with the roller. Peel off the tape when the ink is dry. Create grid square effects by overprinting:

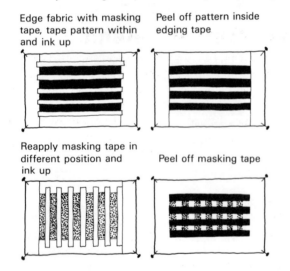

Edge fabric with masking tape, tape pattern within and ink up

Peel off pattern inside edging tape

Reapply masking tape in different position and ink up

Peel off masking tape

Vegetable prints

Additional materials: potatoes, cabbage, iceberg lettuce, carrots, swedes, onions, large knife, lino-cutting tools, pen nibs, small shells, white spirit.

Thin the fabric ink with white spirit. The simplest way of using a vegetable as a printing block is to cut the vegetable in half, ink it up using a paint brush and press the vegetable on the fabric. Refine this by cutting a pattern into a cut potato, carrot or swede using a lino-cutting tool, pen nib or small shell. Avoid cutting out too much of the vegetable. Mark the back of the vegetable to show which way up the print is. The overprinting of colours and the repetition and/or rotation of a simple symmetrical design gives elaborate results:

The washed potato can be kept for a few days in a refrigerator if wrapped in clingfilm. This will allow for overprinting when the ink on the printed fabric is dry.

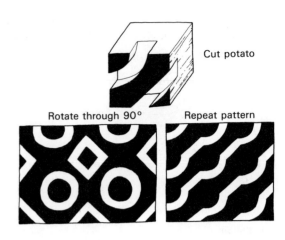

Cut potato

Rotate through 90°   Repeat pattern

Plasticine blocks

Shape some Plasticine into a cube or cuboid. Make patterns in one side by pressing with the end of a pencil. Mark the opposite side of the block to show which side is its top. Paint fabric ink on the pattern on the block and press the block on the fabric. Try overprinting, rotating and repeating the pattern:

PRINTING ON PAPER

Tools and materials

Printing ink, paint, ink rollers, printing trays (or old baking trays), paint brushes (variety of thicknesses), scissors, paper (variety of grades and thicknesses), string, clothes pegs, paper clips.

The techniques described in Printing on fabric (p57) apply equally well to paper.

Preparation

The children should wear overalls (old shirts). Cover all working surfaces with newspaper. When printing with a block, vegetables or found objects, place a thick layer of flat newspapers underneath the printing paper to form a printing base. This will improve the quality of the prints. Cut a number of newspapers to approximately A4 size and have them available for immediately placing over unwanted splashes of ink. Stretch a length of string across the classroom on which to hang prints to dry. Tie knots at equal intervals in the string to prevent prints sliding to the middle of the line. Hang prints using clothes pegs or paper clips.

Card prints

Additional materials: card, cardboard, sheet foam, polystyrene food trays.

Collect scrap card and cardboard from used cereal boxes, kitchen roll holders and other packaging. A polystyrene food tray can be used as a tray for printing ink or paint. A small piece of sponge placed in the tray can serve as an inking pad.

The simplest method is to dip the edge of the card into the paint or printing ink and experiment with the effects from a variety of thicknesses of cardboard and card. Bend or clip the card into shapes such as right angles or circles. Cut a serrated edge into the card and drag it across the paper for interesting effects. Allow the children to experiment with a range of effects.

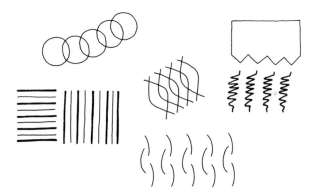

Card printing blocks
Additional materials: card, wax crayons, used Biros, pva adhesive.

Thin card can be used to make printing blocks. Abstract shapes can be used or drawings. Abstract shapes work particularly well when using the corrugations on corrugated card. Draw the main shapes on card, cut them out and glue on a card base in layers to form a printing block. Allow plenty of time for the block to dry. Fine detail can be drawn using firm pressure on the block with a Biro. Place a piece of paper over the block and take a rubbing using a wax crayon. This will give an indication of what the print will look like. Modifications to the block can be made at this stage. Ink up the block using a roller. Place printing paper on the inked block and press firmly with a clean, dry roller (or rolling pin). Peel off to reveal finished print. More than one print can be taken from a single inking.

drawing   Cut shapes glued to card   Ink up block print

Roll paper over block   finished print

Polystyrene prints
Additional materials: polystyrene food trays, used Biros.

Draw the design on the back of a polystyrene food tray using a thick Biro. Ink up the design using a roller. Place the inked tray on the printing paper, applying firm pressure with the fingers. Peel off the food tray carefully to reveal the print. The polystyrene tray can be washed using water and detergent and inked up with another colour if desired.

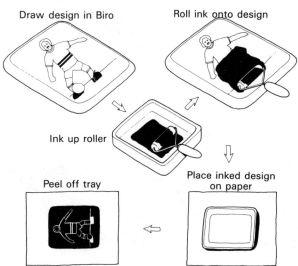

Draw design in Biro   Roll ink onto design

Ink up roller

Place inked design on paper

Peel off tray

Stencilling
Additional materials: greaseproof paper, thin card, masking tape, stencil brush.

Fold a piece of greaseproof paper or thin card in half and draw half of of a simple shape. Cut out the shape, open up and place on the paper to be printed. Secure the stencil using masking tape. Apply paint in a dabbing motion using a stencil brush (for best results) or a paint brush. The paint should be as dry as possible to obtain the best results.

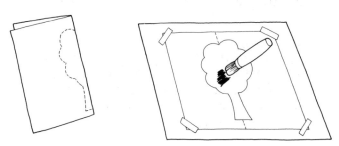

More complex symmetrical designs can be made by folding the greaseproof paper or card into quarters, then making one more fold. Draw the design (curved shapes work well) along the folded edge and cut out along the folded edge only. Open out and follow the procedure above.

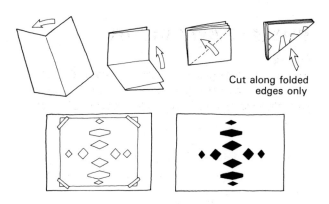

Cut along folded edges only

Borders

Make attractive borders for your prints by laying a thick rectangle of paper in the middle of the paper to be printed and roll or dab paint or printing ink around the edges. Lift up the rectangle and let the paint dry.

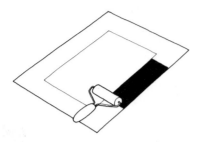

Develop this by making stencilled borders. Cut out a pattern on thick paper or thin card and lay flat on the border. Dab a second colour through it using a sponge or stencil brush.

Any border made in this manner can be made more attractive by overprinting using found objects, vegetable prints, Plasticine blocks etc (see Printing on fabric p57).

 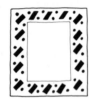 

Cotton reel prints

Cover a cotton reel with a layer of Plasticine. Thread a piece of dowelling through the cotton reel. Make impressions on the Plasticine using a pencil or modelling tool. Ink up the cotton reel by rolling it in a printing tray. Roll on to the paper to create design.

PULLEYS AND GEARS

Pulleys

A pulley is a simple machine consisting of a wheel on an axle with a rope, chain or belt passed over the wheel. Pulling down is usually easier than pulling up. Pulleys make it easier to move loads.

Belts (elastic band, string, wire) mounted on pulleys can change the speed and direction of movement. Such an arrangement is called a belt drive.

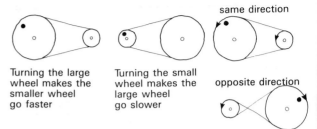

Turning the large wheel makes the smaller wheel go faster

Turning the small wheel makes the large wheel go slower

same direction

opposite direction

Pulleys can be bought ready-made but they can be easily made using cardboard or wooden wheels:

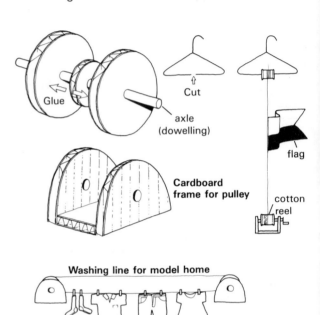

Glue

Cut

axle (dowelling)

flag

Cardboard frame for pulley

cotton reel

Washing line for model home

Pulleys can be attached to a motor to move loads or drive things. For example, cheap push-on plastic pulleys can be mounted on an electric motor.

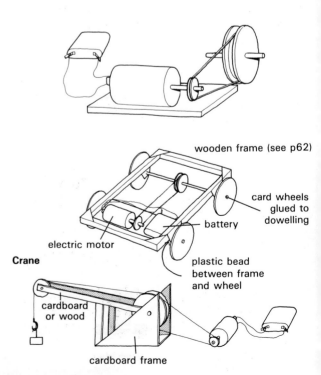

wooden frame (see p62)

card wheels glued to dowelling

battery

electric motor

plastic bead between frame and wheel

Crane

cardboard or wood

cardboard frame

60

Gears

Gears are wheels with teeth which intermesh with other gears. They are used to change the direction and speed of movement. They can change rotation through 90 degrees.

Simple gear systems to demonstrate these principles can be made using coffee jar lids or cheese box lids with corrugated card and dowelling.

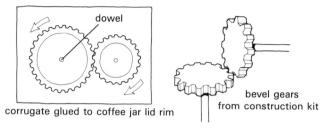

corrugate glued to coffee jar lid rim

dowel

bevel gears from construction kit

Gear wheels can be cheaply purchased. See p62 for further ideas.

Construction kits for work with gears and pulleys: Lego Technic, First Gear, Arnold's Pulleys Science Pack, B tech, Brio Mech, Meccano, Plawcotech. This is not an exhaustive list.

TIE AND DYE

The method described here involves using cold dyes. These are very effective and do not require a heat source. They do not become effective until a solution of salt and washing soda or dye fix is added. The dye solution remains usable for about three hours.

Apart from the cold-water powder dyes (which are cheap and widely available) the process uses commonly available household materials and is simple and fun to do.

Tools and materials
Cold-water dyes (available in small tins), large and small plastic buckets or containers, measuring jug, dye fix or washing soda, salt, large and small spoons, scissors, plastic or rubber gloves, detergent, overall/apron, newspaper, electric iron, string or elastic bands or pipe cleaners, safety pins, clothes pegs, needles, thread, small screw-top containers, dried peas, small pebbles or buttons.

Fabrics: all natural fabrics (cotton, linen, wool, silk) and Nylon. Many other synthetic fabrics take dye well.

Techniques
Use rubber or plastic gloves and protective overalls throughout the process.

For approximately 200 g of dry fabric, dissolve a small tin of cold-water dye powder in about half a litre of warm water. Some of this solution can usefully be stored in small screw-top containers for use on another occasion. If this is done before the salt and fix are added, it will keep indefinitely.

Dissolve four tablespoons of salt and one tablespoon of washing soda or dye fix in half a litre of warm water. Mix the solution in a large bucket and fill with enough water to cover the fabric.

Wet the fabric and fold and tie it.

Immerse the fabric in the dye solution and stir for ten minutes (get the children to take turns). Leave for at least one hour.

Rinse the fabric in a weak solution of water and detergent until the water is clear. Untie the bindings and unfold the fabric. Iron flat whilst still damp.

When the fabric is dry it can be overdyed using different colours and bindings.

water + salt and washing soda or dye fix

Add dye solution, more water and fabric

Stir

Rinse

Folding and tying fabrics
Fabrics are usually more easily folded and tied when damp.

Tie small stones, pebbles or buttons into the folded fabric, using an elastic band to get circular patterns.

Even more complex designs can be made by lightly sewing in lines of small stitches which are pulled up tight, producing dotted lines when dyed. In India, grains of rice are sewn in to make small circles after dying. This sewing process is called Tritik (Javanese for sewing).

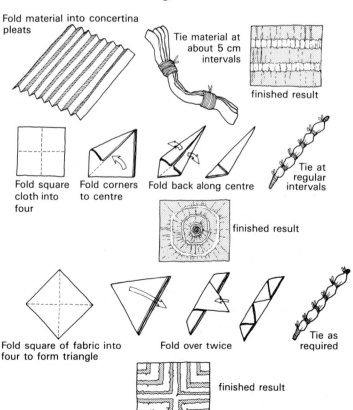

Fold material into concertina pleats

Tie material at about 5 cm intervals

finished result

Fold square cloth into four

Fold corners to centre

Fold back along centre

Tie at regular intervals

finished result

Fold square of fabric into four to form triangle

Fold over twice

Tie as required

finished result

WOOD

Tools and materials

Square cm sections (or 8 mm square sections), dowelling, pva adhesive, bench hooks, bulldog clips, junior hacksaws (or gents saws) hand drill, sandpaper, G-clamps, scissors, card, ruler, wooden or cardboard wheels. Optional: glue gun, drill stand, Lynx jointers, bench hook with cam, lollipop sticks.

Techniques

Insist on the children using the correct tools in the correct manner, keeping the working area tidy. Tools should be put away as soon as they are finished with. Investment in a commercially produced toolboard is worthwhile.

Square cm wood sections are recommended as they are very versatile. They can be cut using a junior hacksaw or gents saw and easily joined with card triangles and pva adhesive. Measure wood carefully.

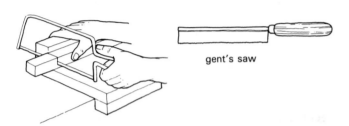

gent's saw

Saw from a standing position. Place the wood to be cut alongside the lip of the bench hook and press down and away from the body with non-sawing hand holding the wood and bench hook securely in place. The hacksaw should be at right angles to the wood or at a slight angle to it. Apply gentle sawing pressure on forward stroke only.

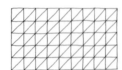

Use the width of the ruler to make grid of squares on thin card. Draw in diagonals and cut triangles.

corner guide

Glue the triangular corner pieces to both sides of the wood joint. A corner guide is useful for lining up the wood at right angles. Use bulldog clips to secure the corner pieces until dry.

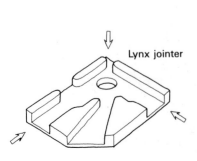

Lynx jointer

Alternatively, use a Lynx jointer. This is useful in making cubes.

Simple designs for buggies

Dowelling is most easily cut using a bench hook with cam. A body for the chassis can be made from card to form a trolley for storing lunch boxes, delivering papers etc. See also Wheels and axles p51.

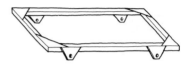

Card triangles with punched holes can serve as brackets for an axle. Take care in lining up the holes.

elastic band wrapped around axle

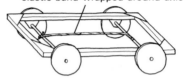
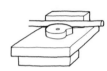

bench hook with cam

Use cubes as a frame for windmills or water mills. This will allow gears to be used.

Watermill

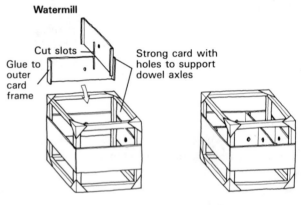

Cut slots

Glue to outer card frame

Strong card with holes to support dowel axles

friction-fit washer

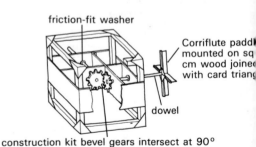

Corriflute paddl mounted on sq cm wood joine with card triang

dowel

construction kit bevel gears intersect at 90°

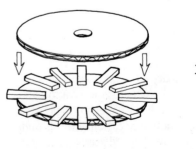
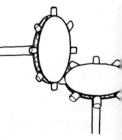

Make gears from card and wood sections, lollipop sticks or dowelling. A glue gun gives the best results. Remember that glue guns should only be used by children under close supervision.

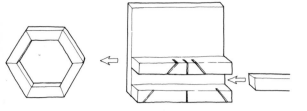

Mitre boards facilitate the cutting of angles.

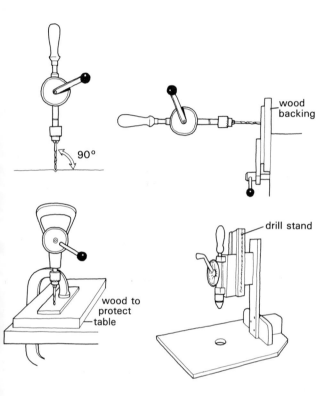

wood backing

90°

drill stand

wood to protect table

Holes should always be drilled from a standing position with the wood held firmly in a vice or G-clamp at 90° to the drill bit. A drill stand can help younger children considerably.

Buggies using different power sources

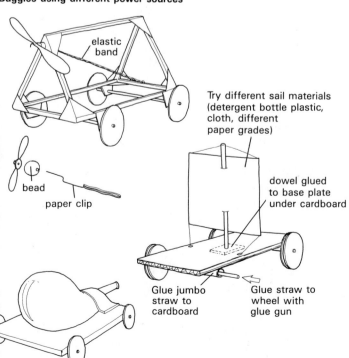

elastic band

Try different sail materials (detergent bottle plastic, cloth, different paper grades)

bead

paper clip

dowel glued to base plate under cardboard

Glue jumbo straw to cardboard

Glue straw to wheel with glue gun

Mobile lifter

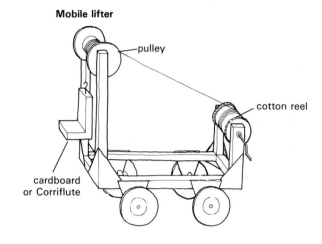

pulley

cotton reel

cardboard or Corriflute

Tower Bridge

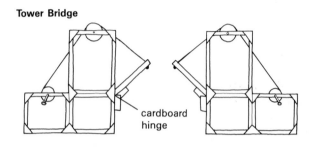

cardboard hinge

Structures and boxes

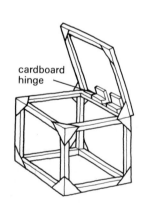

cardboard hinge

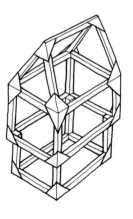

See also Cardboard p50, Wheels and axles p51.

RESOURCES

This is a guide to the basic resources needed for design and technology. Many of the items are commonly available in classrooms. It would be advisable to build up resources slowly, investing in good storage facilities to permit easy access and retrieval of tools and materials.

Graphic materials

pencils	palettes	masking tape	recycled greyboard
paper (variety of book grades)	binding tape	pva adhesive	paper clips
marbling inks	cold-water paste	stencil brushes	scissors
printing inks	wax crayons	felt-tip pens	paints
print rollers	card (variety of thicknesses)	sponge offcuts	brushes
printing trays	large trays		

Construction materials

wood (sq cm or 8 mm sections)	string	lollipop sticks	small pulleys
syringes	electric motors	fishing line	cardboard
3 mm plastic tubing	batteries (match voltage to bulbs)	balloons	dowelling
pipe cleaners		clay	art straws
clothes pegs	bulbs	Plasticine	cotton reels
eyelets	bulbholders	drawing pins	Corriflute
rubber washers	wire	elastic bands	paper fasteners
buzzers			

Construction tools

junior hacksaws	wire strippers	pin hammers	clay tools
bench hooks	single hole punch	wheel punch	rolling pin
metal safety rules	G-clamps	eyelet punch	wooden boards
hand drills	bulldog clips	right-angle jig	wooden slats
craft knives	glue gun	Lynx jointers	safety snips
cutting mats	small screwdriver		

Work with textiles

natural fabrics:	fabric inks	salt	white spirit
cotton	fabric crayons	buckets	detergent
calico	fabric pastels	needles	vegetables (for printing blocks)
synthetic fabrics:	electric iron	thread	print blocks
polyester	cold-water dyes	old blankets	pins
Nylon	dye fix or washing soda	lino cutting tools	buttons

Food

Baby Belling cooker	baking sheet	flour	measuring jugs
measuring spoons	mixing bowl	salt	saucepans
cheese grater	wooden spoon	pepper	kitchen knife
hand whisk	kitchen scales	sugar	forks
breadboard	kitchen thermometer	oil	knives
pastry brush	aluminium foil	margarine	spoons

Junk materials

Challenge the children to design a poster for the collection of these materials:

polystyrene	cheese box lids	shopping bags	yoghurt pots
food trays	kitchen roll tubes	bin liners	corks
cereal boxes	newspaper	milk cartons	used Biro tubes
plastic bottle tops	drinks cans	wire coathangers	Sundeala board
coffee jar lids	detergent bottles	margarine tubs	offcuts

Construction kits

Select one or two of the following:

Lego	Lego Technic 1 & 2	Meccano	Teko
First Gear Plus	Fischertechnic	Lego Control Logo	